THE ADVENTURES OF BUTCH AND RUBY

CHRONICLES OF A CAREGIVER

PRESENTED BY
Dr. Tracy Daniel-Hardy

THE ADVENTURES OF BUTCH AND RUBY

CHRONICLES OF A CAREGIVER

PRESENTED BY
Dr. Tracy Daniel-Hardy

SATURDAY SCRIBBLES, LLC
MISSISSIPPI

Copyright © 2022 by Dr. Tracy Daniel-Hardy

Saturday Scribbles, LLC., P O Box 4071, Gulfport, MS 39502

The Adventures of Butch and Ruby: Chronicles of a Caregiver

ALL RIGHTS RESERVED: No part of this book may be reproduced or transmitted in any form or by any means, graphic, electronic, or mechanical, including photocopying, recording, taping, or by any information storage retrieval system without the written permission of the publisher/author.

For information on booking author for signings, book readings, interviews, and other events, please visit www.saturdayscribbles.com or email tracy@drtracydanielhardy.com.

ISBN: 978-0-578-32834-8

Printed in the United States of America

THE ADVENTURES OF BUTCH AND RUBY
Chronicles of a Caregiver

This book details a year in the life of a caregiver. The ebb and flow in this memoir detail the struggles of Tracy, a primary caregiver, through transparent and entertaining anecdotes. The stories included may make you cry but will certainly make you laugh. The stories may help those beginning their caregiver's journey and may also offer healing and resolve to those who have completed their journey. Each story includes helpful tips generated from Tracy's reflections of her challenges as a caregiver.

Table of Contents

Introduction 1
The Commencement of the Journey 5
Aging Population and Caregiving 10
Introducing Butch and Ruby 12
Home and Neighborhood 27
Neighbors 31
Seeing the Signs 36
Seeing the Signs 42
Business as Usual 44
Find the Beauty in the Ugly 46
Be Watchful for Senior Scams and Fraud 48
Seeing the Signs 50
Take Care of Yourself 54
Seeing the Signs 59
Laughing through the Process 63
Seeing the Signs 67
Seeing the Signs 70

Sand Tarts Recipe...72
Seeing the Signs..73
Seeing the Signs..76
Seeing the Signs..79
R – E – S – P – E – C – T..81
Decluttering..85
I – N – D – E – P – E – N – D – E – N – T.......................................88
Seeing the Signs..90
Seeing the Signs..92
Priorities..94
Seeing the Signs..97
Seeing the Signs..101
Be Realistic about Their Abilities and Limitations......................103
Let Them Be...105
It's Okay to Ask for Help 108
Seeing the Signs..110
Seeing the Signs..112
Change of Scenery...115
Seeing the Signs..117
Be Observant 119
Dementia...122
Seeing the Signs..128
Looking for the Unusual..131
Uncomfortable Conversations..134
Humble Pie 136
Effective Communication..140
Celebrate Wins, Big or Small...143

Seeing the Signs	146
Don't Beat Yourself Up	150
Explain Why (sometimes)	156
Seeing the Signs	161
Don't Take Advantage of Them	163
Leveraging Technology	166
Calling Velma	170
Seeing the Signs	173
That Dang on Truck!!!	175
Be Grateful	181
Conclusion	185

Introduction

My sister and I had a wonderful childhood. We were reared by two loving parents who were always present to support and discipline us when we needed it. They were proud to raise us. They'd prayed for us as daddy often said and continue to pray for us today. They were in attendance and screaming loudly at my baseball games and were the ones shouting orders when I didn't say my Easter speech loud enough for the audience to hear. "Speak up, Tigar!"

I have very fond childhood memories of hanging out with family and friends that we loved at Grandma's house or the home of one of our many relatives. Everybody we spent a significant amount of time with became family and were treated as such. Momma and Daddy always had us involved in whatever they were doing. We helped Momma while she cooked, planted flowers, raked leaves, visited the elderly or sick, and hung clothes on the line in the backyard. I often went hunting and fishing with Daddy and helped him mow the lawn. They both always showed us that they loved us, emphasized the importance of spending time with loved ones, and made sure we could be independent enough to survive on our own.

I particularly enjoyed watching my Daddy groom himself. He was and still is a conscientious groomer. His hair back then had to be combed just right, and his fingernails and toenails had to be cut neatly and were always clean. He still shaves today with a straight razor, as he did when we were younger. He carefully shaves off each hair until his face is as smooth as silk. The process always took over an hour. Once he finished shaving, he would wipe down the entire counter until everything was shiny and spot-free. He still does the same thing today. He ensured that hygiene and appearance were priorities before he stepped out of the house. He made sure that I understood the importance of grooming and hygiene as well. I remember him cutting my hair until he thought every hair follicle was in its proper place. From time to time, he would tell us that "cleanliness is next to Godliness" to make sure we understood that it wasn't just his requirement but that there was also a greater connection to the importance of being groomed and clean.

I always enjoyed being outside doing things with my Dad like cutting the grass, hunting, fishing, and maintaining all the equipment used for those activities. Just like his personal grooming and cleaning, the equipment that we used for hunting, fishing, or lawn care had to be meticulously cleaned and maintained as well. I fondly remember not sleeping the nights before our hunting and fishing trips in anticipation of the excitement of the next morning. As a result of my Dad and the fun I had with him during these childhood trips, I still have a passion for all those things and have shared similar experiences with my own children.

I enjoyed all the things Momma had us do that would help her around the house and that helped prepare us for any life situation. I remember Momma waking us up, sending us to get cleaned up, and calling us straight into the kitchen to help her prepare our meals. Momma thought it was crucial for us to know how to cook, clean, iron, and sew properly. If we didn't do it to her standards because we were slacking off, she would make us repeat the process until we got it right. It was very important to her that we knew how to do those things just right. She also taught us how to be good stewards of the community and the importance of helping those that needed it. It was a humbling experience. I didn't always understand why we did it, but I knew it was important to her. I understand now.

Momma and Daddy also ensured that we understood the importance of faith, family, discipline, integrity, honesty, morals, and values. All those things were instilled not only in my sister and I, but also in all who were at our house for any amount of time, young or old! I am still being taught all these things to this day, not only by their words but also by their actions! They are older and a little feeble now, but they still insist on these values.

Sunday mornings were a time for family and church. We gathered at the dining room table every Sunday morning before going to church. By the time we sat down to eat, we would all be dressed for church or in some stage of finalizing our outfits. We would have helped Momma in the kitchen prepare breakfast and the start of our dinner.

This book details my parents' adventures through the lens of my sister, the primary caregiver to my parents. The book describes some of the daily challenges she experiences with my parents. The book entertains by sharing intimate details of events and struggles with my elderly but independent and comical parents. Words cannot explain or describe my appreciation for my sister's consistent, kind, and loving assistance to our precious jewels. I know it gets hard, yet she continues to be there 100% for them. She has a loving husband that not only supports her but actively supports my parents as well. It's a blessing to have a brother-in-law that loves my parents and is loved by my parents.

The aging process is inevitable and can be both beautiful and challenging. Growing up with strong, vibrant parents was a blessing, and I know that as we age, things will change. However, it still saddens me to see their health decline as they age. I thank God daily for allowing us to be so blessed by the presence of such wonderful parents. I am grateful to God also for blessing us with parents who consistently show appreciation for what we do for them. It gives me comfort to know that they are reaping the benefits from the kindness and efforts they provided to others over the years at this delicate stage of their lives.

They are in their 80s now and have morphed into what I call The Delinquents. They are older, mostly independent, are still strong-willed, but can also be defiant. They are unapologetic about being defiant. They live their lives on their own terms and without much worry. I wouldn't change them for anything in the world.

Enjoy the Adventures of Butch and Ruby through the eyes of my sister, "Dimp," also known as Dr. Tracy Daniel-Hardy.

Andrea "Tigar" Daniels

The Commencement of the Journey

I wasn't ready and felt like I should have been. I saw signs, but I didn't recognize them for what they were. I just wasn't ready and didn't understand what was going on. All of this was temporary, and everything would be back to normal soon—so I thought. Little did I know, this would be my new way of life. I would be required to adapt and adapt quickly. We were all in a new world. The world of Momma ironing all my clothes for the week was long gone, although I was fully capable of ironing them myself. Long gone were the days that often irritated me when Momma would call me at work just to tell me to stop by to get something to eat. We weren't going to see her drive that little silver Nissan Maxima because she never drove again after her stroke. She was forever changed, and so were we.

This was a total disruption. I was well over 40 now and had just found the one. He'd moved here, and we'd begun "living in sin." This was a first for me. I was uncomfortable and worried about what Momma, Daddy, and the good church folk would say. But Momma and Daddy said nothing about it and seemed to be relieved instead of being upset about me "shacking up." They seemed to be smitten with Muhammad just as I was. They, however, struggled to understand his religion (Islam) and his pescatarian diet, but bless their hearts, they tried. They were gentle, inquisitive, compassionate, non-judgmental, and inclusive. Unlike many others, they were and still are the total opposite of Muhammad and what they consider to be his "un-southern ways." I finally felt like things were the way they should be. We were settling in and had begun talking about our forever when Momma had her stroke. This was a total disruption. I needed help with this. My brother was nine hours away in Killeen, Texas, working on his second career as a military instructor and had a child still in school. While he came home immediately, he could not stay for the duration. I needed help. I needed Muhammad to help me with this, but it was not his burden. I didn't know what would happen with us as I needed to focus on my parents. I felt like it wasn't fair to him because he hadn't signed up for any of this. I also felt like it wasn't fair on me to put my life on pause when it felt like it had just come together. However, Muhammad was more supportive and helpful than I could have ever imagined. So much so that he proposed to me in front of Momma and Daddy a couple of weeks after Momma's return home from rehabilitation.

To my surprise, he'd been talking to them about our "forever." He'd evidently told them he wanted to marry me and asked for their approval. On the evening of the proposal, I'd just picked up dinner from Murky Waters (a local barbecue restaurant that serves a great catfish po'boy in addition to great BBQ wings) for all of us. I had given Momma and Daddy their plates while preparing plates for Muhammad and me. In the process of taking out condiments and repacking our portion of the order to transport to our home, I looked up from the bags and saw Muhammad down on one knee asking for my hand in marriage. This was not at all how I imagined it would be. I was surprised and completely caught off guard. I did not have some grand proposal in mind, but I did imagine that it would be in a private setting with just the two of us. Momma had her mouth full of food along with a big grin on her face. Daddy was between bites and had a happy and relieved look.

Several years before the proposal, Momma shared with me that Daddy was concerned about me. He'd asked her, "Is that girl alright down there?" He had been worried about me for some time. He was bothered by my unmarried status and how I was living alone. He was overly concerned with my safety and happiness even though I was in a long-term relationship at the time. Momma and I found a way to find joy and laughter in that, as we have traditionally done with so many uncomfortable and unfortunate events. I asked her to always respond to Daddy's question or concern about me with a "No, she's not alright. She needs money!" We continued to laugh and moved on to the next conversation. I was elated that Daddy was relieved because I was getting married to someone he liked and trusted. He could now stop worrying about his "baby girl."

Muhammad and I planned a small, intimate wedding in three months with the assistance of a few friends and family members. My cousin Mavis styled my hair. Cherise, my former student and celebrity makeup artist, gave me a soft natural face beat. My dear friend

Robin officiated and kept the nuptials respectful of Christianity and Islam. My high school friend and college roommate, Nikki, who is talented, creative, and frugal, was our wedding planner and decorator. Cedric "CC" Tillman, our college classmate, was the wedding photographer. My secretary, Hope, and her husband catered the event and prepared our honeymoon food basket.

Muhammad's parents, my parents, brother, best friend Dana, her family, and a handful of other close friends and family joined us for the mid-week wedding. The ceremony and reception event was short and sweet. Both were held in the same room at an event hall and not in my church as I'd always imagined. Muhammad's talented Uncle Harold drove down from Atlanta with his teenage son to entertain us by soulfully playing the guitar. He played beautifully. We danced. We laughed. We took pictures with all our guests and enjoyed each other. Uncle Winnie and my late Uncle Junior each shared a sweet dance with me to support their brother, my Daddy. It was such a memorable moment.

Hope, my secretary and wedding caterer, had prepared our honeymoon picnic basket to take with us to the Jasmine Suite at Beau Rivage Resort and Casino. She had packed up the leftover food to send home to our house with Muhammad's parents who were staying with us.

Our guests snacked on popcorn (Muhammad's favorite snack) and cookies from Quality Bakery as they waited for the wedding ceremony to start. Our cake was a delicious and simple, two-tier almond cake prepared by the same bakery.

By December, when the wedding occurred, Momma was doing better. However, she was still talking very softly, moving slowly, and adjusting to her life after the stroke. We were all adjusting. Daddy had to do more than he'd ever done before, and Muhammad and I were adjusting to our new roles as newlyweds and senior caretakers.

I didn't marry until I was 45 years old, but I still carried those expectations of roles into my marriage that I witnessed in my parents' marriage and the marriage of other family members. I expected my husband to drive me on road trips just as Daddy did. I was appalled when Muhammad began to pack separately as we prepared for our initial trips. I expected that we would do as my parents did and pack together. I did not expect Muhammad to be a BBQ grilling man as Daddy wasn't. I still find it interesting that Muhammad has never expressed a desire to purchase a truck or attempted to buy one. We always had a truck. I guess it's an old southern thing because the men needed a truck to haul materials and fishing and hunting gear.

Muhammad, my husband, is from the Midwest, where the expectations of husbandly duties may be different from those here in the south. His expectations are not wrong. They are just different. It's possible that his self-defined expectations were formed by the different cultures he has lived around. He didn't subscribe to the man driving the family and owning a truck duty expectation like the men in my life did. He was very independent and self-reliant instead of relying on his wife to cook, clean, and pack. Here in the south, the roles are pretty defined. Muhammad and I did not stick to those designations. As I suspect that most successfully married people do, we expressed our own expectations.

Aging Population and Caregiving

The aging population of the United States has grown by over 34% since 2010 to 56 million. In contrast, in 1963, only 17 million members of the United States population were 65 years old or older, according to the United States Census Bureau (http://www.census.gov). According to the Administration on Aging, the number of aging adults (65 years and older) is expected to grow to 98 million by the year 2060. The older adult population, aged 85 and older, is projected to double by 2040. Additionally, older women outnumber older men by 6 million according to the 2017 Profile of Older Americans. Since 1900, the population of older Americans has increasingly grown older and is expected to continue to grow older until at least 2060. Women are also likely to outlive men by two and a half years. There were 92,000 centenarians (100+-year-olds) documented in 2020, an increase of 10,000 from

2016. According to the United States Census Bureau, the population of adults 100 years old and older is expected to grow to 589,000 by the year 2060. Over half of those being cared for live at home, nearly one-third live with those caring for them, and less than five percent are in some assisted living facility.

Nearly 12% (40 million) of the population of the United States are unpaid caregivers like me to aging adults or adults with disabilities. According to the National Council on Aging and the National Alliance for Caregiving, these caregivers are typically women approaching 50 years old (like myself) who have teenage children or grandchildren and maintain a job along with other responsibilities while caring for an aging adult. Data show that the health of caregivers can suffer up to three years after the end of the caregiving journey. Caregivers also develop more chronic illnesses, fail to monitor their health, have poor eating and exercise habits, and are more likely to show symptoms of depression (National Alliance for Caregiving).

Like myself, many of these caregivers have been thrust into the caregiver role with little or no preparation or training to explain how to adequately care for the aging adults they are responsible for. The journey can be simultaneously daunting and rewarding. Travel with me on our journey of caring for Lucious and Ruby, my parents, who are also affectionately known to many as Uncle Butch and Aunt Ruby.

Introducing Butch and Ruby

Momma and Daddy have a loving marriage. Daddy was the protector and very much the man of the house. We were taught to respect him and his word. Momma was the disciplinarian, the fun one, the MacGyver (because she fixed everything), and the homemaker. She cooked, cleaned, sewed, and ironed. Mom was still ironing my clothes when she had her life-changing stroke. She'd iron the clothes that I'd washed, hang dried, and dropped off to her every couple of weeks or so. She'd iron them up and call me when they were ready to pick up. A few times after her rehabilitation and adjustment to her "new normal," she ironed a few clothes for me but lost interest in continuing our arrangement. I think the task became too great for her due to her decreased stamina.

Daddy fished, hunted, and cut the grass, but he didn't even attempt to fix the car or tinker with faulty electronics because, in his words, "they had professionals to do that." He, nor our neighbor,

Gary, were the typical Southern dads to grill on the weekends. There was no grilling from those two houses on our street ever.

Momma took great pleasure in waiting on Daddy, and he enjoyed letting her. Momma and Daddy thought that I would do the same with my husband. Daddy even tried to encourage it, offering hints and nudges. However, they were wrong. It's just not our dynamic. We have specific things that we routinely do for each other instead. However, Muhammad just might disagree with my description of our relationship.

When we took trips as a family, Daddy always drove. There was a defined process. Daddy picked out his clothes, and Momma packed the clothes. Momma was also supposed to double-check that Daddy picked out everything he needed for the trip, including undergarments, toothbrushes, and other personal items.

We always had a truck and a car. Daddy drove the truck. Momma drove the car. When we took family trips, we always took the car. When Daddy and my brother went hunting, or the whole family went fishing, we rode in the truck. I remember the blue Ford F150 or 100 truck, the red Ram truck, and the black Cordova that Momma drove forever.

ABOUT RUBY

Momma has always had a hearty appetite. She loves to eat and takes her time savoring each bite of her food as one would expect of a heavier woman. When she was pregnant with me, her first child, she was approximately 96 pounds. Right now, at 116 lbs., she is the smallest that I've ever seen her in person. (I've seen the maternity pictures of her). Even at 116lbs, her appetite is still hearty but waning. She has lost some interest in foods she previously enjoyed. Her desire for these favorite foods seems to come in waves now....no chicken one month while having a strong desire for it another month. She has been consistently avoiding fried shrimp and has recently expressed that she's had enough fish for a while. Both fried shrimp and fish were things she'd always enjoy and could eat at any time. However, she cannot seem to ever eat enough Blue Bell's vanilla ice cream or the very southern "cornbread and milk" side dish I've watched her eat all my life. I think the wavering desire for food is a symptom of her dementia, as many who suffer from dementia lose interest in food and eating. It could also be simply due to changes in smell and taste because of the aging process.

I remember when Momma was actively trying to gain weight and had grown to a plus size 14. She was thrilled about her weight gain. Unlike many women today who want to be slim and trim, Momma always wanted to be plump. For some reason, she liked stoutness. She even told me that she liked me "round" as opposed to when I'd lost a bit of weight and was less full-figured than I am now. That flabbergasted me, but she never did sugarcoat anything.

I'm not sure from where her desire to be plump emerged. Maybe it was simply because she was always smaller, very much like how women who have naturally curly hair want straight hair and vice versa. It could simply be her unique preference. I am not sure.

Momma wasn't and still isn't a glamorous or fancy woman. She was and still is rather conservative and modest in her appearance, beliefs, and character. She doesn't wear makeup or pants (except workout gear or pajamas) but instead favors A-line skirts, colorful and straightforward blouses, and flip-flops or sandals. She has this simple beauty that blossoms when she laughs. She enjoys being domestic. She loved cooking, gardening, cleaning, and taking care of her husband and children. She is sad that she cannot cook, clean, garden, and support us in the same fashion that she could before her stroke. She is a country girl at heart.

Momma was known for her domestic skills. Today, she is still known for her homemade biscuits, salmon croquettes, and chicken and dumplings. The chicken and dumplings dish was often the preferred meal cooked for and delivered to bereaved families in our community. It was also the requested dish for her to bring to potluck events like church programs, family gatherings, or reunions. Although she "lost" the desire to cook homemade biscuits when quality, pre-prepared, frozen biscuits arrived in local grocery stores, she never lost the ability to make those savory chicken and dumplings. She can still make them from scratch, as she has always done if my brother or I are in the kitchen helping her. Helping her looks like one of us just hanging around close to her in the kitchen and maybe fetching something at her request. Our presence gives her confidence and prevents her from walking away from the kitchen and burning the food.

Momma enjoys simple things. She likes sewing and cooking, thrift stores and gardening, animals and babies, sweet potatoes, parched (roasted) peanuts, pecans, "cornbread and milk," and ice cream. She loves teaching and training others on the basics of domestic tasks. She likes to walk you through cooking a particular dish or mending a piece of clothing based on the fabric and cut of the garment.

When my brother and I were growing up and even after I left for college and he left for the military, there were usually parched peanuts on the stove, ice cream in the freezer, corn flakes in the cabinet, and during the fall, there would be baked, sweet potatoes resting on the stovetop. Those were our snacks. We didn't have a lot of chips and cookies in the house as is commonly on counters or in cabinets in many American households today.

My brother and I, along with our cousin Mark (who is like our brother because he spent a great deal of time at our house), and anyone else who might have been visiting us, had to cook and clean. If Momma was cooking, cleaning, or working in the yard, we were too. Everybody at the house (except Daddy) helped out. Momma made sure that we knew how to do everything. We all (except Daddy) helped prepare our meals. We each had a task. My brother was typically the butcher. He had to cut up the chicken. Mark's task was to prepare the banana pudding or dessert when he was there. When he wasn't there, it was my job. I remember being in charge of the vegetables. I would be responsible for cutting the corn off the cob to prepare fried corn or cutting and preparing the okra, squash, etc. Momma taught me how to shave the corn off the husk gently and thinly before scraping the remaining corn "milk" in a pan to be seasoned and fried in a little bit of vegetable oil or bacon grease, to make the fried corn dish we loved so much.

We were not allowed to wear wrinkled clothing out of the house. Momma made sure we knew how to iron clothes properly. We learned that shirt sleeves and jacket sleeves should be ironed differently. She even made us iron all of the family's clothes for the week. Not just our clothes, but we were required to iron the clothes of everyone in the house. I hated that practice and still do today. I do not iron my clothes for the week as she trained us to do. I've tried, but it just doesn't work for me.

Respect was not optional. We were taught to respect our father as the head of our household. We had to take care of him. We ran his bathwater. We laid out his T-shirt and boxer shorts on the bed to put on after his bath. Momma made sure that what Daddy picked out to wear was ironed and lint-free for him to put on. He took meticulous care of his shoes and taught us how to care for ours using a well-stocked shoebox that he still has.

We not only cooked dinner, but we also fixed Daddy's plate and walked it to him. If he wanted seconds or anything, we fetched it for him. We picked up his plate when he was finished eating and took it to the kitchen. I hated how Momma made us wait on him. She took great pleasure in being attentive to Daddy and making sure that we, too, were attentive to his needs. She was even attentive to our wants and needs, much like she was with Daddy's needs. Although she made sure we knew how to cook and clean, she enjoyed waiting on us as well by ironing up our clothes, fixing our plates, etc., after she made sure that we'd mastered those skills.

We learned how to thread a needle and thread the sewing machine, hem pants, and skirts, mend holes in clothes, layout clothing patterns, and cut fabric. I didn't know how to buy a dress until I left for college because Momma had made all my dresses and skirts before then. We would even buy skirts or dresses that caught our eye only to take them home to use as a pattern for our own version before returning the unworn garments to the department store.

Momma is one of 16 children (12 girls and 4 boys) born to Elijah and Georgia in the Darbun Community of a small town outside of Hattiesburg, Mississippi. She is the oldest and longest-living member of their immediate family today. Momma and her siblings are Clara Mae (deceased), Timothy (deceased), Rosie Mae (died as a child), Ruby Lee (Momma), Edward (Elbert), Georgia Marie (deceased), Selena, Modine, Bert, Avis, Alice, Hamp, Bertha Lee (deceased), Grace, Brenda, and Rufus (deceased).

Momma shared that she and her family were poor farmers in one of the many rural parts of Mississippi. They were a loving and hardworking family. Momma remembers only going to school on rainy days because those were the days that they could not farm the fields. She has fond memories of cooking, sewing dresses from flour sacks, and helping take care of her siblings and the farm animals. She affectionately speaks of her father. I remember him driving down the narrow roads of her hometown with his hand out the window, waving to everyone in sight. I also remember her mom, who Momma remembers as always being pregnant. My memories of "Grandma Georgie" are pleasant and sad. Memories of her cooking in the kitchen on the old stove, giving herself insulin shots, and having her hair styled in two, long plaited ponytails that resembled an American Indian as she sat wheelchair-bound from what I believe was a stroke. I remember her smell. She had a strange, sweet smell that I now know is a classic sign of uncontrolled diabetes. Grandaddy, too, had diabetes. As a side effect of his diabetes, he had very sensitive feet (diabetic neuropathy) and would cut holes in his soft bottomed mesh-like shoes to allow some relief from his discomfort. They, too, were kind-hearted people.

My grandparents were known as good, hardworking people who had many children (16 of them). Grandaddy drove a school bus. I never knew if Grandma Georgie worked anywhere other than in the home. I can't imagine her working another job and caring for her husband and 16 children. I remember taking the short hour and a half drive that seemed too long, turning onto Bethlehem Loop and driving forever until we turned off in front of the family church before arriving at my grandparents' home. I remember their first home looking like something from an old movie. I remember a small, old wooden structure that wasn't painted was slightly elevated with a front porch, tucked away in the woods. My most profound memories are of the new, brick home with the big garden, hog pen, chicken coops, the full clothesline hanging grandma's house dress and grandaddy's overalls, the wonderful smell and popping embers of the fireplace during wintertime, and our big family gathering together during Christmas.

ABOUT BUTCH

Daddy's skin is a very rich, dark umber color. He is a handsome and charming man who is incredibly particular about his things. He diligently cuts his nails and spends a great deal of time filing and cleaning them. His hair combing routine is equally meticulous. Daddy has a beautiful smile and a beautiful, soulful singing voice. He can almost pray you straight into heaven with his spirit-filled, long prayers. (My cousin Mavis would often look at me while at church during one of his long, spirited prayers to jokingly tell me to get him because his prayer was taking so long.) He's a deacon in our church and has been since the late 1970s, although he hasn't been active since Momma's stroke. (When Momma began to stumble more, he decided not to leave her home alone to attend church.) Daddy used to hum a lot. Actually, he used to hum all of the time. When all was quiet or when he was in deep thought, he would hum. He would stick to the same run of 3 or 4 spiritual songs. It was annoying yet calming, depending on when he did it. Now that his short-term memory is fading, he hasn't been doing it as much. After not hearing him hum at all for a year, he began humming a little more recently.

Momma always made sure (and still does make sure) that Daddy's clothes were neatly pressed and hemmed. Daddy made sure his shoes were always dust-free and well-polished because of the well and always-stocked shoebox he had all my life. He made sure that my brother and I understood the value of clean, well-polished shoes too. We had to clean and polish our shoes using the correct shade of shoe polish, the right shoe rag, and the perfect brush for the cleaning and polishing process. Shoe polishing became a bonding activity between Daddy, my brother, and me.

Daddy was meticulous about grooming and was known for taking a long time to bathe and shave, using a straight-edge razor blade. Those close to him would often joke about it, especially if they stopped by the house to visit and he wasn't available because he was shaving. They knew that he would not be available to visit or chat for a while. We also knew we wouldn't be able to use the one bathroom we had in the house too.

Daddy was also very particular about the care and use of his equipment. He was not one to loan his lawnmower or weed eater to a neighbor or friend because no one would care for their equipment as he did. Immediately after every use, Daddy would spray down the lawnmower and weed eater and clean the blades. Once they were carefully cleaned and oiled, he would neatly place the lawnmower and weed eater in the garage so that no other equipment or items would touch or damage them.

Daddy was born in 1938 to Eddie Mack and Lena Bell in Selma, Alabama. Selma is the home of the Edmund Pettus Bridge, where the Bloody Sunday Selma to Montgomery March happened on March 7, 1965. I always had an eerie feeling when we drove across that bridge during a visit to Selma for a family reunion or funeral. In March 2020, I visited Selma to commemorate that awful Bloody Sunday with thousands of my sorority sisters. I had the same eerie feeling walking across the bridge as when I was a child. I imagined how those walking in protest for their inalienable rights, mentioned in The Constitution, felt as they were beaten on that very bridge.

Daddy was one of eleven (11) children born to Eddie Mack and Lena Bell and one of twelve (12) (including a cousin, Uncle Ben) raised in Alabama and later moved to Gulfport, Mississippi. When Daddy was 18 years old or so, Grandma Lena Bell gathered the children and left my granddaddy to move in with her uncle in Gulfport. I loved my granddaddy dearly but was told that he would often drink too much and become violent. I never witnessed it, but everyone told similar stories about him. To protect herself and her children, Grandma Lena Bell left my grandaddy in Selma, searching for a safe haven in Gulfport.

Daddy and his siblings are Mack (deceased), Iantha, daddy,

Ruthie, Lorraine (deceased), Rosilyn (deceased), Margaret, Alice,

Rosemary, Wendell, Mass Mack (deceased), and Cousin Robert

McCord, Sr. (Uncle Ben).

I was really close to Grandma Lena Bell (Daddy's mother). She was a short, petite lady with a raspy voice who was a great cook. She often shared family stories as we cooked together or sat and drank coffee together at the dinner table. Grandma Lena Bell's dining room table (and home) was always open to guests. Drinking coffee and eating Sunday dinner at Grandma Lena Bell's table were popular events. Grandma's table was the gathering place for the church deacons, clergy, family, and anyone needing a bite to eat or a place to stay. Decisions were made and relationships were formed at Grandma's table over coffee, a meal or cake, and surrounded by cigarette smoke.

I remember cooking yeast rolls and ham with Grandma Lena Bell (not necessarily at the same time). She taught my friend, Gretta, and me how to make pecan candy (pralines) correctly, emphasizing the patience needed for the process. Grandma told tales of my beloved grandfather getting paid, getting drunk, and becoming mean. I learned that witnessing that made my Daddy swear off drinking and made him despise when any of his siblings drank alcohol because he feared they would act like his father.

According to Grandma and others, the young women would line up at her uncle's house (their new Gulfport home since leaving Selma) looking for Daddy and his brothers. They were the new, very handsome, and talented dudes in the neighborhood. All but the youngest brother sang well and quickly joined or formed singing groups. (Ironically, the youngest brother, Uncle Junior, had three daughters that could sing very well.) That made the new Alabama boys even more attractive, as I'm told.

Momma was of the holiness religion (Pentecostal), and Daddy was Baptist. My brother, Tigar, and I attended the holiness church with Momma until Daddy became a deacon at his church. I remember Momma and Daddy having a conversation about attending separate churches. I distinctly remember Daddy saying, "the family that prays together, stays together." Shortly after that, we joined Daddy at his church. We still attend and are members of that church today.

Momma's church was very charismatic with lots of loud music, holy dancing, tambourine thumping, and long services that scared my brother and me to tears. We were happy to be attending Daddy's church, but Momma was not as excited. She was like a fish out of water because the church services differed so much. She seemed bored during church service and often slept in church even until she stopped going after her stroke in 2016. The church service in the Baptist church was milder and a lot less energetic than Momma was accustomed to.

Momma became a deaconess, as is expected of a deacon's wife in our new church (Daddy's church). She also became a junior choir matron and is still known today for having maintained order in the choir, as no other matron had been able to do. I remember Momma and Daddy regularly visiting the sick and shut-in at the hospitals, nursing homes, and their homes. They spent hours each week (often on Sunday evenings) visiting the sick, elderly, and bereaved, praying for them and providing company, comfort, and sometimes food. Other hours during the week were spent at choir rehearsal, Bible study, prayer meetings, deacons/deaconess meetings, or at our games. I played softball, and my brother played baseball.

Momma was known as a great disciplinarian who loved children. She could get the children to learn anything or do any chore. She did not tolerate disrespect or disobedience. She would spank you and "love on you" simultaneously. She is still known to give a look that will straighten up the most disruptive child (and adult). From this special skill, she began babysitting a few children. Some because they requested her to, while others she volunteered to keep because she felt there was a need to help. These children were well-disciplined, well-fed, and loved Momma and Daddy as if they were their own grandparents. They called them Aunt Ruby and Uncle Butch or PawPaw.

Daddy now spends much of his time in bed or sitting out back, killing ants with his walking cane (He uses the cane to kill ants, not to assist with walking. Many years ago, he had back surgery and used the cane then.) He drives a clean 1978 silver and black Ford truck and takes several trips around the neighborhood daily in it. Some say they can tell the time of day by his trips down their street or past their homes. The truck has a very distinctive sound and can often be heard when he passes our house on the opposite end of the same street.

When Daddy is in the house, he can sit and watch sports television, hunting shows, Wheel of Fortune, and the news or stay in bed all day. One would think that he hears nothing when he actually hears everything. He chimes in unexpectedly or much later about something that was said when we thought he wasn't listening. He doesn't answer the house phone unless you hand it directly to him and tell him to answer if it rings. He often leaves his cell phone on the end table next to his chair in the living room. So, we must go out back to find him if we need him or want to see him.

Daddy used to fish a bit when we were younger. We would all go fishing on the rock-piled pier at the beach, not far from our house. He was an avid hunter, preferring to hunt deer, unlike his brothers, who preferred rabbit hunting. My memories of Daddy going deer hunting in the winter consist of him coming home with those big, heavy snake boots, thick hunting suits on, and my brother and I pulling his boots off. The boots were so heavy and difficult to take off that my brother and I would fall back to the floor once we rocked forward, then backward enough for them to break free.

Daddy would leave really early in the dark morning hours to go hunting and return in the early evening of the same day. I remember hearing the distinctive sound of him stepping onto the wooden-planked back porch with the heavy boots, rustling overalls, and the tired moans as he neared the back door of the house, where I greeted him with "Watcha kill, Daddy? He'd often reply "Time!" because deer hunting was quite different from rabbit hunting. When he went deer hunting, he often sat in a treehouse, waiting and sitting as still as possible for a deer to appear. When he went rabbit hunting, he would always come home with rabbits they'd killed. When he went deer hunting, he'd only bring home deer a third of the time.

Daddy retired from a construction company when I was in college. Momma worked as a hairstylist for many years at my aunt's (Cousin Mark's mother's) beauty salon named after her, Rosilyn's Beauty Salon, where the slogan was "We curl up and dye for you." After working in the beauty salon for many years, Momma worked at South Mississippi Regional Center. The South Mississippi Regional Center is a center for individuals with mental retardation. She retired from the regional center and initially started babysitting (by request) for a few close friends and relatives.

THE MEETING

Daddy and Momma have been married over 55 years now. Yet, as the story is told, Momma and Daddy met at a local radio station (WGCM) near Turner's Cafe in Gulfport, Mississippi. Turner's Cafe was a popular cafe in Gulfport before I was born. Daddy was in a singing quartet with several other guys including one who happened to be friends of Momma. The quartet was broadcasting a show at the radio station when they realized they needed directions to get to their next gig in the Tylertown area. One of those guys knew that Momma was from that area and contacted her for directions. She met them at the radio station to share directions. Momma and Daddy were introduced and began dating shortly after the meeting.

They dated several years before getting married in March of 1966. After five years of trying to conceive, Ruby and Butch had their first child, Tracy (me), in 1971. That was a particularly rough time for Momma because her sister Bertha Lee and Bertha's new husband were killed in a car wreck in Momma's hometown of Tylertown, Mississippi. Thirteen months later, my brother, Andrea "Tigar" was born. Momma and Daddy recall visiting the doctor, concerned that I was no longer accepting Momma's breast milk. To their surprise, the doctor informed them that Momma was three months pregnant with my brother.

Daddy had two other daughters before he and Momma were married - Joyce, who lives in the South-Central Region of the United States, and Brenda, who lives in southwestern Mississippi.

Home and Neighborhood

Our neighborhood is a low to moderate-income neighborhood with 40% of its residents renting homes. Our street is a quiet street with a handful of school-aged children and many older and elderly neighbors. Many the residents on our street have been there for many, many years. Some residents have inherited their homes from a deceased relative, and others are renting from the families of deceased relatives who previously lived in the homes. There are several empty and unkempt lots on our street and in our neighborhood. Many of these vacant lots on our street held homes that Hurricane Katrina ravaged in 2005. A few of the lots have what appear to be weak structures standing and in a blighted state, while others are empty with overgrown fields. We have inquired and complained about the blighted properties only to hear from city officials and city workers of a long, ineffective process filled with red tape.

My parents' home was built in the early 1920s, as I discovered in 2020 while filing an insurance claim for roof damage caused by

Hurricane Zeta. My parents purchased the home from the Adams family, who attended our church and lived a couple of streets over and next door to my best friend, Dana, until they both passed away. The home survived Hurricane Camille in 1969. Momma and Daddy rode out Hurricane Camille tucked away in the bathroom of their home. Hurricane Camille was the worst hurricane to hit the Mississippi Gulf Coast prior to Hurricane Katrina and the second most intense to hit the United States. It was classified as a Category 5 when it made landfall on the Mississippi Gulf Coast. According to the National Weather Service (weather.gov), it is still one of only four hurricanes to make landfall in the continental United States as a Category 5 hurricane. According to Weather Underground, Hurricane Camille made landfall on the Mississippi Gulf Coast near Waveland, Mississippi, with 175 mph winds (after reanalysis), making it the second strongest hurricane to make landfall in the history of the United States. (The first was the Great 1935 Labor Day Hurricane that made landfall in the Florida Keys at 185 mph winds after reanalysis.)

The home has endured Hurricanes Camille, Frederick, George, Katrina, Zeta, and other smaller, less impactful hurricanes. While some would categorize the home as small, it is sturdy and always filled with love. The three-bedroom house is equipped with a closed-in front porch, living room, dining room, back porch, and one bathroom that we made work for our family of four. The front bedroom was my bedroom but was my parents' bedroom of choice after my brother, and I left for the military and college. The middle room was my brother's room and has now been converted into an ironing room with lots of clothes and shoes everywhere. The back room was Momma and Daddy's room. It was the guest bedroom and was the spot where clothes were tossed after being brought inside from the washer and dryer housed in the garage.

Since Hurricane Katrina, the garage has been full of stuff and can no longer serve its original purpose. After Hurricane Katrina, a small addition was added to the garage to house Daddy's truck. Momma still walks out the back door, down the stairs, and through the backyard to get to the garage to launder clothes.

The backyard still has a clothesline that is rarely, if ever, used. We used to use the clothesline all the time. Momma especially enjoyed hanging the clothes in the springtime to dry. Once Daddy finished mowing and edging the lawn, he would clean his equipment under the clothesline.

There is a saucer magnolia tree in the middle of the backyard. It's in an awkward position, but Daddy had to have a magnolia tree in our yard. There is one variety of our state tree (saucer) in our backyard and a Southern magnolia tree in the middle of the front yard in another very awkward spot. After the magnolia tree in the front yard grew tall, the grass no longer grew and was replaced with big, fallen magnolia leaves.

A few years after Hurricane Katrina, an orange tree grew from the orange seeds Momma tossed out in the backyard on the south side. Several years ago, it began to produce lots of tasty oranges. One year Momma and Daddy had a genius idea that would allow them to get to the oranges at the very top of the tree where they were "plentiful," as Momma would say. They borrowed a taller ladder than Daddy's from their neighbor, Mr. Vernon, and arranged it on top of their ladder. Daddy's friend, Mr. Roy, walked up from behind the garage just in time to see the dangerous situation. He warned them, but they didn't listen, and the ladder toppled down with

Daddy on it. Daddy landed hard atop Momma, who was holding the ladder(s) for his security. They both landed on the ground. He hurt his hand and arm while Paige (the little girl Momma was keeping at the time) was wailing in fear that they were badly injured.

Hearing each of them tell the story made me laugh hysterically and prompted me to buy them a few fruit-picking tools. Daddy was still getting on top of the house at 80 years old, picking oranges from the tree while Momma picked the lower-hanging fruit from the tree. The oranges were not very pretty, but they were bountiful and sweet.

Neighbors

We have always been blessed with great neighbors. On the south side of my parents' home is Mr. Vernon (Daddy's personal mechanic, so he thinks) and his wife, Ms. Mary. They moved into Aunt Mamie's house in the 1980s, a few years after Aunt Mamie died. Aunt Mamie was an older widow that wasn't our aunt but watched after all of us as if we were her nieces and nephews. Mr. Vernon and Ms. Mary have three wonderful daughters that are several years younger than my brother and me. I didn't get to know them well before moving away to college. However, Mr. Vernon and Ms. Mary are lovely and considerate to Momma and Daddy. They always keep a watchful eye for Momma and Daddy.

On the other side (the north side) of Momma and Daddy is the home of Gary and Lenoira. Gary is the oldest brother to my best friend, Dana. Gary and Lenoira moved into their home a couple of years after Mr. Bud and Mrs. Lizette, the previous neighbors, passed away. Gary and Lenoira raised five children in that home. Tomeaca, the nurse who advised Momma during her stroke; Candace, the teacher; Gary, Jr., the entrepreneur; Jeremy, the teacher and coach; and Selena, the baby of the crew. I think they moved into the house next door in the early to mid-1980s. They have always been good neighbors and are really helpful with Momma and Daddy. They do more than I will ever know that they do. Daddy takes great pleasure in watching their driveway to see when the kids come home to visit and when the grandchildren are over there. Daddy and Momma expect the grandchildren to come to visit them and catch them up on what's going on in their lives.

Across the street from Gary and Lenoira is Grandma Lena Bell's house. Grandma Lena Bell was Daddy's mother. My cousin, Eve, and her daughter, Jayla, her son, Christian, and Eve's cousin, Trimaine, live in what we still call Grandma's house. Although Grandma has been gone for over a decade now, we still call it Grandma's house. Momma was babysitting Christian at the time of her stroke. He was two years old then and full of more than average boyish energy. Momma and Christian have the cutest, special bond. He is always looking for her outside, and she is always looking for him when she is outside or passing by their house. Eve and the kids are always helpful and loving towards Momma and Daddy, keeping a watchful eye on them. If something is not right, they check into it and handle it or call me.

I am very grateful for having great neighbors. They are not just the ones close by like Mr. Vernon and Ms. Mary and Gary and Lenoira. But also, Jean and Lil' Luke, who are next door to Grandma's house, and Aunt Jean and Mrs. Reed, a little farther down the street. Lil' Luke and Momma also have a special relationship. Lil' Luke is an adult with gray hair but will always be Lil' Luke to us.

Many years ago, Momma taught Lil' Luke how to play dominoes and jacks, go job hunting, and cut his hair when he was young. He still keeps an eye on things when he's around.

We all still yell, "HEYYYYYY!" down the street or up the hill when we see each other. If we are riding by, we slow down to wave and smile to acknowledge each other. Momma and Daddy's sitting spot in the house is situated so they can look out the north window and see Gary and Lenoira's driveway, Grandma's house, and Jean and Lil' Luke's house. If they are actively looking out the window, they can even see whose car is driving past.

Our street is tight knit. Most of us attend the same church located at the end of our street. It is one of the larger churches in our area and has an aging congregation and a traditional model of Southern Baptist worshipping. The membership is dwindling a little bit due to having an older congregation and a very traditional service. However, we have some great, active youngsters who sing in the choir and are part of the mime and praise ministries.

I look at my parents and see a much smaller and fragile version of those who raised us. I remember noticing the more fragile versions of them at first and crying. They were no longer the strongest people I knew. They had become feebler and more complacent. Daddy seemed more acceptant of the new version of himself while Momma ventured over only after fighting like hell to avoid it. She went down kicking and screaming. She was distraught. She often cried because she lost something that she was very proud of, her independence, which gave her great pleasure in the ability to help others. Momma has a faithful servant's heart. Seeing her engaged in this fight was probably the saddest thing I've ever witnessed so intimately. It was as sad as, if not more tragic than, watching my dear Uncle Junior take his last breath.

According to their doctors, my parents' brains have shrunk. Just thinking of that process makes me cringe and become upset. The significant brain shrinkage (brain atrophy) that typically begins around age 60 contributes to age-related dementia. It's like any other mechanical equipment. Some just naturally break down for a variety of reasons - the quality of materials from which they are made (human heredity), their exposure (human environmental factors), and the usage and maintenance (human lifestyle, diet, and health and fitness).

My parents were not social butterflies. They were church social, if that counts. Their social activity mostly involved church activities, church events, church people, and family. I think Momma is the extroverted one (as is my brother), and Daddy is the introvert as I am. Momma loved getting out to be around people before her decline. However, after the stroke impaired her independence and made her appear very fragile, she avoided those same things she once enjoyed. She tried but soon stopped. I don't think she liked the attention she got during her ventures. People flocked to her because they were happy to see her, but they talked pitifully to her. They ran to assist her and spoke to her gently. They no longer saw her as the caring disciplinarian who did much for others. She was now one of those who she would have tended to by taking them home-cooked meals, helping them clean or do yard work, and fixing their hair.

I don't remember the day, but I remember noticing a change as she seemed to accept the inevitable and settled into her new, less independent role. It seemed as if her mindset changed. The crying stopped. The antidepressants helped with the crying as well. The help that the antidepressants provided was not authentic like her new mindset was. The confidently crossed legs with the head held high suggested that she'd embraced the new version of herself and accepted the newfound ways she could still feel useful.

Seeing the Signs

There is beauty in the whole process if you open your eyes and look closely enough. After I stopped crying the sad tears so much, I saw things differently. I saw that God granted new talents, gifts, and opportunities amidst the challenges of recovery and aging.

Momma had a stroke in early August 2016. I remember the day pretty vividly. My husband and I were traveling when I received a call from Momma to tell me that she thought she was having a stroke because one side of her body felt like it had "run out of gas." I felt helpless because I was six hours away from her. However, I've been given the ability to think calmly and quickly during difficult times. So, I quickly devised a plan. I told Momma to get Daddy up out of bed and go to the emergency room. I also began calling close friends and family who were nurses to get guidance and my best friend to act as my proxy since I was out of town. Momma was unbelievably calm and got Daddy up without alarming him too much to take her to the hospital. After getting there and being briefly examined, she was told by the emergency room physician that she was dehydrated and was subsequently sent home to rehydrate. When we talked again shortly after that diagnosis, she expressed that she still could not sit up straight, had slid off the toilet, and could no longer walk upright or sit upright. I called my childhood friend and former neighbor, Tomeaca, who is a nurse, to ask for professional advice. Her instructions were to tell Momma to go back to the emergency room and insist that they perform a cat scan of Momma's head and be persistent in describing her symptoms.

Tomeaca sent her parents (Momma and Daddy's next-door neighbors) over to check on my parents. At the same time, I called my best friend, Dana (Tomeaca's aunt), to go with my parents to the emergency room to ensure the hospital staff did not send Momma back home without the proper tests and a diagnosis that made more sense. I hesitated, but I also called my very aggressive but get-it-done friend, Gretta. I knew Gretta would clown should something go awry, but she would also question things, take good notes, and keep me updated often. Dana and Gretta made me feel as calm as I could be under those circumstances.

The hospital admitted Momma after the test results showed that she not only had a stroke but had had a series of mini strokes in the past. (When she thought she'd had a stroke a few years prior because her mouth became twisted, she had probably correctly diagnosed herself then also when the doctor told her that she was simply suffering from Bell's Palsy.) Momma stayed in the hospital for a couple of weeks. She cried so much and so hard because she was so afraid of losing her independence, not necessarily about dying. It was the saddest thing I'd experienced. It was horrible. I felt helpless. Although we tried reminding her often that she was very blessed to be alive and to have as much control of her body as she did, it did not stop the tears. She cried when we walked her to the bathroom. We had to stand there with her and hold on to her to keep her from tumbling off the toilet. We had to help wipe her while she cried even harder. We had to get in the shower with her to bathe her. She cried and cried uncontrollably during each of those activities for the entire hospital stay. We cried when she cried. Her little nose would turn so red and snotty that you couldn't help but feel sorry for her. The staff cried when she cried and when we cried. It was all so sad.

After spending nearly two weeks in the hospital, we decided on rehabilitation. We wanted her to use the rehabilitation services provided by the hospital just a couple of floors away from her hospital room, but insurance would not approve. This, I believe, was the official start of my caregiver's role. I researched facilities that her insurance approved and decided on one that was not at the top of my list but was on Daddy's list. Daddy selected the facility because it was very close to our home and the hospital. I visited the facility and became even more uncomfortable with the selection, but I respected Daddy's choice and moved forward with the process of securing a spot for Momma there.

I felt so unequipped and ignorant when I spoke with the social worker during the rehabilitation enrollment process. I knew very few answers about their insurance. I didn't understand Medicare or Medicaid but gave her the correct answers based on her description of the programs. I was frustrated that I didn't know more about their business. Before then, I had no reason to know that information, so I thought. I didn't know about their medicines and very little about their health because they were generally in good physical health.

We were questioned about assets and properties to determine if we qualified for Medicaid. Although my parents did not qualify for Medicaid, I learned that the Medicaid qualification would allow a longer rehabilitation stay since Momma's insurance only allowed a stay of 20 or 21 days. We chose the private room option and made the room smell and feel cozy as possible since we would spend at least 20 days there.

I grabbed one of many notebooks I kept and began to take note of every person and conversation I had with rehabilitation center staff. I questioned everything that I didn't understand and repeated what I thought I understood to them to confirm my understanding. I asked questions to make sure I understood the process and that they were following the established plan for Momma. Also, it all needed to make sense to me. According to Momma, the staff was very careful with her because they didn't want to upset me. They told this to Momma when I showed up during her bath one day. They'd rolled her back into the room from her shower, and I'd noticed her demeanor was off, and her face was in a frown. I questioned both the nurse's assistant and Momma about the cause of Momma's disposition. Momma would not tell me what happened until after the assistant left. The assistant had carelessly wet Momma's hair with cold water. This upset Momma every time it happened (even when I did it) and caused her to shiver whenever it happened. Momma told me that the staff was very concerned about upsetting or causing her discomfort because they didn't want to make me angry. This baffled me because I'd not displayed anger with them but questioned many things and wrote down everything. I didn't mind them being extra cautious with my mother but didn't want them to fear me.

I was pleased to find out that the director of the physical rehabilitation portion of the center was a former middle school cheerleader of mine. Because of that, she took special care of Momma and her treatment. She made time to answer the many questions I had. I discovered that she was the director from Ms. Amy, who works in the pre-school department upstairs from me in my building at work. Someone mentioned to Ms. Amy that Momma had a stroke, and Ms. Amy tracked me down in the building to express her concern for Momma and ask questions about her stroke and treatment. I found out that day that Ms. Amy was a little saint. She worked well with little ones, but also spent many of her weekends at Momma's rehabilitation center and other similar facilities providing therapy. Ms. Amy even worked with Momma on one of those weekends and made a memorable impression on Momma and Daddy. She offered several exercises that helped with Momma's rehabilitation, and she checked on Momma from time to time.

Momma continued to cry even when going home after spending two weeks in the hospital and another two weeks in the rehabilitation facility. I didn't realize that the doctor had prescribed antidepressant medicines until I started administering her medications. At the time, I thought if the antidepressants were working, her sadness (depression) was much more severe than we thought. Trying to avoid crying when around her took great effort. Momma is a doer and a helper. She did almost everything for Daddy and many things for me and others in our community and within our circle of friends and family. The stroke made it impossible or very difficult for her to do those things. The dynamics of her relationships with others changed. Daddy, who is spoiled, began doing things for himself that Momma always did for him. He stepped up to do things for

Momma that she could no longer do for herself. My brother and my relationship with Momma changed to that of caregiver. It encompassed the parental role that Momma always held for not only us, but for our cousins, friends, and neighborhood and church children. Momma was always the caretaker. Now, Daddy, my brother, my husband, and I had become her caretakers, and nobody liked it. We wanted things to go back to normal, where she took care of us.

She has not driven a vehicle since the day before the stroke. Momma was always on the go. Her car sat in the back of the garage until 2020 during the middle of the COVID-19 pandemic when my brother and I purchased it from Daddy for nostalgic reasons instead of selling it to someone else. Momma was also babysitting Christian when she had the stroke and could no longer babysit him. She missed his company and their special bond. She always enjoyed cooking but could no longer stand long enough to cook a meal. She couldn't organize her thoughts to manage the preparation and task without being distracted, confused, or growing weak and tumbling to the floor. She also enjoyed doing yard work and gardening but could no longer stand long enough or physically move as she previously could before the stroke.

Seeing the Signs

Don't ignore the signs. Mood changes and sustained irritability can predict medical issues that may be occurring.

As I think back to the time before Momma's big stroke, I noticed a change in her mood. It reminded me of Ouiser in the movie Steel Magnolias when she said, "I'm not crazy, M'Lynn. I've just been in a very bad mood for 40 years!" It was not quite as long as 40 years, but sometimes it might have been as bad as Ouiser's mood. Momma, who has never had a problem speaking her mind, became even more outspoken and was very irritable. Her tolerance for things that didn't normally bother her, bothered her greatly. Daddy might have been catching it at the house too. He'd buck his eyes, nod his head at me and say "UhmmHmm" when I'd seem shocked at something uncharacteristic that Momma said or did.

Those were signs of hormonal changes and indicators that something else was happening. We could have discontinued estrogen use, which might have attributed to the strokes, or we could have taken her to talk to someone like M'Lynn suggested for Ouiser in Steel Magnolias.

Business as Usual

Mom doesn't manage her meds, but she calls in Daddy's refills. She still takes great pleasure in being his secretary, and we let her.

As I've previously mentioned, Daddy is very spoiled. Momma takes great pleasure in waiting on him. One of the many roles that she has always assumed is the role of secretary. She has always written the checks, paid the bills, prepared the tithes for church, called in his prescriptions, dialed the phone to call people for him, and reminded him of necessary appointments and events. Since she takes pride in doing all of these things that he can do for himself, we call her his secretary.

Interestingly, the stroke and general aging have caused cognitive impairment. It seems only to impact what she needs to do for herself. The cognitive impairment is not very evident for what she has traditionally done for Daddy. It is amazing to see. Ask him if he has taken his medicine. While he pauses to think, Momma answers without hesitation, even while doing something else like eating or walking. Ask her if she has taken her medicine, and she has no clue if she did or not. Sometimes Momma just says yes, when she has not, but is simply remembering when she has taken her medicine a few days before. Whenever he needs refills on his medicine, she calls Walmart to request the refills. When she needs refills, she says nothing and will let them run completely out. Her glucose sensor will stop reading, and she will just sit it down, stop using it, and won't tell me about it.

Even though she has difficulty standing for a while, she still irons Daddy's clothes and does a bit of mending to them when needed. She has brought in a stool that is situated ideally for her to iron and hang the clothing afterward. The space that she irons is not very safe because everything is within reach or hung closely. She doesn't have to move about much however, I worry about her falling because there is so much stuff in a small space.

She still remembers how to cook but cooks very little because she will forget that she's cooking and burn the food or get tired and fall in the kitchen from standing too long. But she still does pick what Daddy eats and prepares his plate or gives him the plate and gets him something to drink to go with the meal that has been prepared for them. Momma still prepares his coffee every morning. Daddy says that she sometimes forgets, but she disagrees. He sometimes forgets that she has made it for him as the prepared coffee cup sits on the kitchen counter.

Find the Beauty in the Ugly

There is a camellia tree in my parents' front yard that I don't remember being there during our childhood. Momma got a "piece" of a camellia tree from the yard across the street from their neighbor after they departed. She also has white roses, yellow roses, white azaleas, light pink azaleas, a magnolia tree that Daddy planted, hen and bitty plants (actually called hen and chick plants), and many other plants that I can't name.

As you can tell, Momma loves plants rather than flowers. She saw the beauty in flowers but did not like their fragility and their short-lived beauty. She preferred the longevity of plants. She still has plenty of plants that she cares for, but something new started a few years after losing independence. A fresh-picked flower was placed in a plastic cool whip bowl on the table. There were sometimes yellow roses but would most often be these beautiful camellias. I finally asked who picked them for her. She gave me the stern surprised "Ruby look" and said "ME!" while pointing to herself. We laughed as usual, especially after telling her how pretty the flowers were and how ugly the bowl was. Then, I asked her to pick one of the beautiful flowers for me the next time she picked flowers. She did. It seemed as if she carefully selected the most colorful and fullest red camellia on the tree for me. She was proud but not nearly as proud as I was to place the vibrant red flower in my bright yellow, happy face mug on my work desk. The flowers seem to give her more pleasure now than the plants...not just any flowers, but the flowers that are fruits of her labor. How beautiful is that!

One of my neighbors gave me a plant. Many of the leaves were burned on the ends. I watered the plant often and watched as new shoots emerged to have burned ends too. I kept with my process of watering and pruning. I got the same results. I decided to ask the plant doctor, Momma, what was wrong with the plant as she walked toward the kitchen in my home. She stopped and barely glanced at it, replied, "You are overwatering it," and continued her stroll into the kitchen. So, I stopped watering the plant as much and noticed the difference. The new shoots grew normally with no burned tips. I didn't ask her why the aloe vera plant that I have in the kitchen windowsill was not flourishing as it once was. So, I stopped watering it as much and saw the same result. The aloe vera plant is now growing more as well.

It's incredible how Momma and Daddy remember so much about things that I have never known and forgotten.

Be Watchful for Senior Scams and Fraud

Many seniors get caught up in games of chance and donation schemes sent by mail. Please monitor their mail and bank accounts for any evidence of these schemes. The $5, $8, $11, etc., donations to fake and legitimate organizations as well as games of chance can add up to hundreds of dollars per month pretty quickly.

Daddy's not a gambler and even avoids going to dine at casinos because of the gambling there. But he was caught up in the mail schemes that promised significant returns for a small $5, $8, or even $11 investment. These people or companies continued to send enticing letters with promises of potential cash rewards if the recipient sent another small investment to secure the "deal." Once I realized that Daddy was deeply entrenched in the schemes and was consistently "investing," I talked to him and warned him about those letters.

The seniors may even start to purchase money orders if you limit their ability to write checks or when they find out you monitor every transaction as Daddy did. Once there were no more checks to write, to my surprise, Daddy went to the bank to purchase money orders to continue sending money to the schemers. If I didn't see it myself, I would have doubted that it even happened. He walked in the back door to the living room with it in his hand. He saw me and was disappointed that I witnessed him give it to Momma to complete the money order and place it in the envelope to mail.

He did not stop his involvement overnight. It required several conversations and even one threat to pull in my good friend, Kim (an attorney) to discuss it with him before he complied with my request to stop investing time and money. Although he still receives communications by mail and he may even open the mail from these scammers, he has not (to my knowledge) sent any more money to them or replied to their messages.

Seeing the Signs

Consider obtaining power of attorney for your aging parents to manage their finances, medical needs, etc.

Having the power of attorney will authorize you (the agent) to speak or act on their behalf legally. Choose carefully what type of power of attorney you create - financial, healthcare, or both to ensure you obtain the rights you need to assist them effectively. The financial power of attorney allows the agent to manage financial transactions. The healthcare power of attorney gives the agent the ability to make medical care decisions for them should they no longer be capable of doing so.

Being added to their accounts and knowing the company representatives they deal with is not always enough to take care of business. Be respectful of the senior's wishes and consult them and your sibling(s) before making big decisions to ensure everyone agrees.

The first time I used the Power of Attorney was to dispute a $495 charge on one of their bank accounts. Once the bank representative reviewed the Power of Attorney and my identification, conducting business on their behalf was a breeze.

After being added to my parents' bank accounts, I began regularly monitoring their accounts through the banking apps to identify opportunities to reduce spending and pay bills. During my regular review of their accounts, I noticed an unexpected charge of $495 from a company I was unfamiliar with. I questioned Momma and Daddy on a couple of different occasions over the weekend that I noticed the charge and in a few different ways. Doing that often-yielded better results and could jar a memory that they didn't quickly remember. Their stories regarding this transaction never changed. They had no idea about it. I searched the company's name on the web and called the number attached to the transaction. The results made me question the charge even more. I tried disputing the charge by phone over the weekend but could not do so by phone. Each bank representative I spoke with by phone told me that I had to conduct the dispute in person at the bank. That Monday morning, I went to the bank to do just that. Having the Power of Attorney and being on the account made it a simple process that did not require me to drag my parents to the bank with me to resolve the issue.

The fees for Power of Attorney can include an attorney fee, notary fee, and optional court filing fee. However, you may have friends who can take care of this for you for minimal cost or no cost, as I do.

Prior to the unexpected charge, Daddy had asked me to step in to help with finances after receiving an overdraft notice on one of the accounts. When we visited the banks to add me to the accounts, I noticed some unexpected challenges and opportunities with their accounts and spending. As I began to work on those issues, I was asked a few times by company representatives if my parents were available to verify the change request or if I had Power of Attorney. After going through that process several times, I asked for help from my good friend, Kim, an attorney. She sent me several versions of the Power of Attorney to help me decide which best fit our needs. After selecting a format that met our needs, I left the Power of Attorney sitting on my dresser for several weeks because I didn't like taking the necessary steps to begin administering their financial affairs. In my mind, it meant admitting what I still did not want to accept – my caregiver role. I talked with my brother about it. He and our parents agreed that we needed to move forward with the Power of Attorney. But, it just felt wrong to me. Their memories and capacity to manage bills and finances had diminished and required my assistance since my brother lives away in Texas.

We prepared the final documents for each parent and handed it to them for a final review and to affix their signatures to three copies that were also notarized.

The process was pretty simple because of Kim's guidance. If I didn't have Kim, my friend of over 35 years, I would have had to pay an attorney to guide me through the process, draft the Power of Attorney and pay a notary or risk using an online template to develop my Power of Attorney documents.

Guardianship and Conservatorship should also be considered. There are times when one may need to secure guardianship instead of power of attorney. Both power of attorney and guardianship allows someone to act on behalf of someone incapacitated. However, power of attorney is appointed by the incapacitated, and the guardianship is granted by the court to be the decision-maker for someone who has been deemed unable to make sound decisions and/or unable to take care of themselves. Similarly, a conservatorship is granted by a court to someone to manage financial affairs on behalf of someone who cannot do so (usually someone who suffers from dementia, mental disability, or some other serious illness). Obtaining guardianship and conservatorship is more intense and expensive than obtaining power of attorney. Guardianship and conservatorship applications require (in my state of Mississippi, at least) one to obtain documentation of the incapacitation from doctors to present to the courts. The courts then will carefully consider what is being requested while protecting the rights of the vulnerable.

Take Care of Yourself

You are no good to anyone if you don't first take care of yourself.

Failing to self-care is also failing to care for those in your care.

Disconnect from those high-stress things and find things that relax you.

Accept help if you need it or want it!

Find people and/or services that will help you (meal prep, meal deliveries, housekeepers, etc.)...anything that will help you and those in your care. Love on those you are caring for and yourself! A colleague from Charlotte-Mecklenburg School District mentioned, on a panel on which we both served, that you have to put on your oxygen mask first. We are specifically told to do this by flight attendants before the airplane leaves the terminal. I have learned through this process that I am most present, make better decisions, and am more alert when I have engaged in self-care. Other times, I am just operating on fumes and just going through the motions.

Like my husband and I, many caregivers have other responsibilities, including working a full-time job. Unlike us, many caregivers often have a family of their own to manage. My husband and I do not have children to manage, but we have many civic and social obligations to which we have committed. This often means coming home to go straight into a meeting for at least an hour, planning and attending events, working on committee reports, graphics, websites, etc. for several hours, organizing and scheduling meetings around work and caregiver duties, taking numerous calls, and responding to many emails. It feels very much like my husband and I each are working three full-time jobs.

I've learned to pay attention to my body, mentally and physically, and mind my calendar. When I am mentally or physically exhausted, and my calendar of events is light, I take a mental health day. Recently, I took one that did not include answering the phone or responding to text messages related to work. It was wonderful. I slept, made and ate breakfast, watched tv, slept some more in a different location in the house, surfed the web and social media, and showered before my husband made it home from work. I was refreshed, wide-eyed, and bushy tailed. I did not drag into work the next day. My mood was better. I was a better listener and reasoner and gave things my full attention, unlike it had been for the prior couple of weeks.

It also made me less frustrated with my parents and what I needed to do for them. Even though I've learned to respond more positively to my parents, I know they can feel when I'm sincere or not. It's better for all of us when we can bring our genuine, open, and helpful selves to our duty station.

The Adventures of Butch and Ruby

PRIORITIZE SELF-CARE

I was preparing to cook a breakfast of pancakes, bacon, grits, and eggs recently one Saturday morning for us, my parents, and my brother, who was in town visiting. Usually, breakfast does not consist of pancakes and grits. However, my husband and I wanted pancakes, and my brother always requests that I prepare grits and eggs each morning of his stay when he is in town. When bacon is on the breakfast menu, I always begin cooking the bacon first because it generally takes longer to cook than the rest of the meal. After lining the sheet pan with foil for the bacon to cook in the oven, I realized that I had not purchased more bacon. I was out of bacon. There was none in the fridge and none in the freezer. The crazy part about that discovery is that I'd moved one pack of bacon from my parents' refrigerator to their freezer just the day before because I noticed that I'd overstocked them with bacon.

This revelation made me pause (after I called my brother to bring me a pack of bacon from my parents' refrigerator) because my over preparation for their house and the under preparation for our house has become common. It has become too regular of an occurrence. I'd also previously noticed that we'd run out of sodas and bottled water, but I'd made sure my parents had enough of both to last at least a month. The revelation was that I was prioritizing their care over mine. I'm aware that many caregivers act just like I have done. They take better care of those they care for than they do themselves. Often chores and home repairs are left undone at the caregiver's home while those same things are meticulously done at the home of those they care for. Changes in behaviors and health are shared with the doctor about the one being cared for, while the caregiver's health often declines because the caregiver fails to make the time to maintain regular doctor's appointments.

I cannot promise that I will master taking care of myself and my home as I do for my parents, but I can put forth a concerted effort to do so. So, I ask my caregiver friends who are reading this to vow with me to avoid neglecting themselves. Additionally, to those who are friends or family members of caregivers, please encourage and remind the caregivers in your life to prioritize self-care and avoid sacrificing their household for the sake of their caregiving duties.

Caregiving can be a stressful job. However, it can also be very rewarding to care for someone who once cared for you. What's even more rewarding, though, is prioritizing self-care and ridding yourself of stressors that can make you ill or incapacitate you. Caregivers must put on their own oxygen masks first. Doing this helps guarantee that there is a bit of "self" left to give to others, often helps improve the caregiver's quality of life, and allows the caregiver to provide better care to those for whom they are in charge.

According to the caregiving statistics, most caregivers are women 49 years old or older. Many of those women work full-time jobs or have careers while juggling a family of their own. I am pretty sure that many of those individuals find themselves constantly worrying. They may even lack the ability to remember things or have problems concentrating because they are in a constant state of overload. Some of those same caregivers may even abuse alcohol, drugs, and/or carbs or find themselves constantly irritable, short-tempered, angry, or on a retreat from society altogether. These are all the results of stress.

I suggest that caregivers (or anyone) identify what stressor elimination looks and feels like for themselves. Some may find stress elimination in removing themselves from a toxic work environment, getting out of a toxic relationship (spouse, courtship, entanglement, friendship, or a commitment to an organization that doesn't align with your values or passion, etc.), or simply setting boundaries for people and things.

Stress elimination is not easy, especially if you are used to being in a constant state of stress. Know that when one begins the stress-eliminating quest, the resistance will rise. The people, organizations, and institutions that benefit from the stressed individual will start to stand up to request that you continue your journey with them. When this occurs, cover your eyes and ears and stay the course of self-care through stress elimination. Your brain and body may even begin to rebel against you because they are used to being in a state of stress. Stay the course even then. Like people and organizations, your brain and your body will adapt. Doing this offers you a better quality of life and may even extend your life.

Identify what relaxes you and commit to doing that thing routinely. Be selfish sometimes and go to the spa for a massage, facial, manicure, or pedicure. Sleep in and watch television. Go fishing and running. Sit on the beach and watch the tide roll in. Explore your creativity by painting. Read a book or two. Go to the movie theater or sit on the front or back porch and enjoy the breeze.

Take time to care for yourself.

Eliminate the stressors and don't feel guilty about it.

Put on your own oxygen mask first!

Seeing the Signs

Please seriously consider getting your 65+ loved ones and those with pre-existing health conditions the COVID vaccine. COVID is more deadly now than it was when we stayed in the house and took more precautions eight months (or so) ago.

I took my parents to get the first dose of the vaccine in March 2021, during the time everyone was scrambling to find vaccination sites in Mississippi. Daddy took his vaccine like a champ. Momma...well, she took hers...uhm...not so much like a champ. She whimpered a little bit. Muhammad and I had been earlier that morning to get our vaccinations. Before leaving, I was able to grab two sets of paperwork to take with me to fill out for them. I got both their signatures on the forms before returning to the site with them to get their shots. Doing that made the process very simple. They allowed me to take both of them to one makeshift room with black curtains instead of sending them to separate rooms in the community center where the vaccinations were being given. I watched

Momma's expression because I expected her to be a little animated. As the nurse prepared Momma's arm for the shot, I began shaking my head at her because I could still see the "Aunt Ruby" expressions even with a mask on. It was the stern look of disapproval with the frowning eyes that she would give to her nieces, nephews, children in the choir, children in her care, and any child acting up. The look she gives includes looking you straight in the eyes and telling you to straighten up without actually saying a word to you. The look may be accompanied by her big index finger pointing at you in a quick, repetitive motion. (It could also be a finger point with just a wag, or it could be that finger-pointing in the direction that you needed to go to complete the straightening up process.) Momma furrowed her brow and shook when the nurse gave her the shot as if the nurse was intentionally hurting her. During the 15-minute "vaccine reaction" wait, we were quietly cutting up (she and I, not Daddy). I was trying not to laugh out loud at her as the nurse said to me with a silly smirk in her eyes, "Oh, I'm sorry! I'm sorry! I'm sorry!" If you know them, you know Daddy was just sitting over there, not saying anything, and shaking his head at his silly girls.

He did have plenty to say later about the long wait for our food, though. It, obviously, took too long for him as we sat in the truck waiting.

Momma and Daddy both have pre-existing conditions and are well over 75 years old (the magic age for priority vaccinations). This placed them in the high-risk category for complications should they contract COVID-19. Momma has diabetes and hypertension, while Daddy has hypertension.

Before the pandemic, my parents had lots of visitors. So many people "love on" my parents by visiting just to chat with them and bring food, snacks, and supplies. After the state of Mississippi's "Safer at Home" orders were issued by our governor because of the increasing COVID-19 cases, I had a talk with Momma and Daddy about visitors, wearing masks, and sanitization. After talking to my brother and healthcare workers, I placed a sign on the door that informed everyone my parents were not accepting visitors unless it was the home health nurse or therapists. The sign also gave instructions for dropping off food and supplies to them. I made and bought masks for them and talked to them about the importance of being safe and staying at home as much as possible. They acknowledged my declaration but did not fully comply. Daddy hadn't considered that getting his weekly haircut was a problem. He also thought it was okay for Dana's kids (my best friend's children) to visit and hug. (They told me that Daddy told them the sign was not meant for them.) We had to have several conversations before he completely understood how important it was for them to adhere to the rules. Eventually, the severity of everything sank in, and they complied, mostly. My little cousins still visited. Christian was only three years old, couldn't read the sign, and needed his snacks from "Wu-by" and "Uncle Butch." The rules did not apply to him. He was always in and out quickly. Rarely did he linger long after saying hello and getting his snacks.

When the number of positive cases began to drop, I changed the sign to allow masked visitors. At that point in the pandemic, my husband and I wore a mask EVERY single time we visited my parents. We were still working around people who were not always taking necessary precautions or other people who were not precautious. We were cautious. We avoided crowds and stayed home as much as possible ourselves. We did not hug or kiss them for a year. We elbow-bumped them and blew kisses to them for a year.

Once we all received our second dose of the Moderna vaccine, I was excited. All four of us received our first dose on the same day but did not get the second dose on the same day. Momma and Daddy got their second dose a week after us. After the two-week period expired after our first dose, we stopped wearing the mask when we visited them and started back hugging and kissing them. I remember the first hug and kiss. Momma hugged me so hard and so long that I wanted to cry. On the other hand, Daddy said, "Who told you it was okay to hug and kiss now?" while still allowing me to kiss him. They both love hugs and kisses. Due to their love for hugs and kisses, I explained that others still needed to wear masks when they visited them because not everyone was fully vaccinated. Although I told them they shouldn't hug and kiss other people, I know they would not remember or comply. I constantly prayed for God's protection over them and us.

Laughing through the Process

It was a cool fall day in South Mississippi, with temperatures around 50 to 60 degrees with very little to no humidity. It was cool enough to wear a sweater and boots, but some were dressed in shorts and sandals. Momma and Daddy were dressed like it was freezing and had the heat set on the "hell" setting as usual. This day, as on most fall days, the house was so hot that I began to sweat as soon as I walked into the living room from the front porch. While I was sweating, they were bundled up and comfortable. Momma was wearing her nightgown and fluffy blue terry cloth robe, Daddy's old, big hunting socks, and her gray slippers. Daddy was dressed in a pair of his neatly pressed blue jeans, long sleeve button-down plaid shirt buttoned up to the neck (always with an undershirt on), and his natural-colored Kenneth Cole casual dress shoes. His natural-colored leather jacket was close by, so he could quickly grab it on his way outside to sit for a spell or take one of his many rides around the neighborhood.

Don't forget to laugh through the process. We get through it by laughing a LOT. (Well, Momma, my brother, and I laugh a lot. Muhammad tries not to laugh, and Daddy just shakes his head at us.

Me: "Here, Momma, you didn't take your meds today. DADDY!!! (Me yelling), did you take your medicine this morning?!"

Sassy Momma: Nodding her head in the affirmative and saying yes as if I'm talking to her.

Me: Looking at her with my hand on my hip and with my head cocked to one side...."Oh, you know when he takes his medicine, but you can't remember if you've taken yours."

Sassy momma: Laughing and laughing while nodding yes again.

She rarely forgets to fix his coffee whenever they decide to get up and does not forget to iron his clothes but doesn't care ANYTHING about remembering to take her meds.

Laugh!

IT'S OKAY TO LAUGH AT REALITY

As I imagine most do, my parents' insurance encourages a yearly in-home wellness visit. Well, we've been missing the calls to schedule the visits because Momma and Daddy don't answer the phones. They get many calls, mostly healthcare scamming calls (don't get me started on that). Although I know that the scammers spoof local numbers and other recognizable numbers to trick us into answering their calls and listening to their spill, I answered the phone when I heard the phone announce their insurance company's name. After exchanging greetings, introductions, and a little laugh (Me: Hi, I'm Mr. Daniel's secretary), we set up a wellness visit for the 23rd.

Yesterday, Jessica (the nurse practitioner) called to see if she could visit that day instead because she had a few cancellations and was in the area. I took a deep breath when she asked that because you all know that could cause an issue to get Daddy to get up and move quickly. So, I told her that it would be fine for her to visit if he was up. While she and I chatted, I dropped in on the cameras to see where Daddy was. I started with the bedroom camera and quickly went to the living room because the bed was empty. Both Momma and Daddy were seated in the living room. Daddy was dressed in his jeans, colorful socks, and white wife-beater t-shirt. Before agreeing to the visit, my next concern was to make sure that Jessica would receive accurate info because I couldn't leave the office to meet her there for a visit. I told her that she could visit if she promised to follow up with me afterward to get the real story. I knew they would simply tell her everything was fine while grinning big. After agreeing to the follow-up call and ensuring she could access Daddy's medications, she was on her way to see him.

She called, as promised, after her visit and started the conversation by saying, "I visited them, and they are so precious." (I blushed because I knew how true this was.) She corrected herself and said that she had just visited Daddy. Then she began to give me a rundown of the questions, answers, and observations. I wasn't surprised when she said, "Your mom stood up nearly the entire time I was there." Before she finished the statement, I interjected to explain Momma's role. I told her that Momma was 'The Supervisor' and that's what supervisors do. Jessica laughed and let me know that eventually, Momma got tired and did sit down.

After telling me what she asked Daddy and what they told her, I verified their responses. Most were accurate and on point. Then

Jessica mentioned that part of the visit's purpose was to ensure the patients had heat and air. She may have said something else also, but I didn't really hear that because I was laughing. That check of "heat and air" made me chuckle. I said to Jessica, "Yeah, I guess you know the heat works, huh, because it's hot as hell in there." She laughed awkwardly before replying, "Yes, it was working, and with my mask on, it made it really hot!" We had a good laugh together about that before she let me know that she was used to experiencing the heat.

Jessica verified that Daddy was doing well and concluded the call by setting up Momma's visit since we'd surely missed the calls to schedule hers.

Laugh, y'all! According to Ruby Daniel, a good laugh, similar to a good cry, is like taking a "good dose of medicine."

Seeing the Signs

Allow extra time for senior appointments to ensure they are ready and can enjoy the ride.

I have found that allowing an extra 45 minutes to an hour reduces frustration for my parents and me. I used to have it timed perfectly to drive up, run in to grab them, get them buckled up, and speed off to the appointment. That rarely worked and resulted in having to rush them frantically. However, I had to adjust because I didn't like how that disrupted their calm dispositions.

Momma and Daddy's memory is not what it used to be. In all honesty, neither is mine. I'm almost 50, as Daddy takes great pleasure in reminding me. I use Google Calendar religiously with notifications and alerts a week, day, and even an hour before the appointment. From our collective lack of memory, I have to tell them about appointments several days in advance, ask them to repeat what I told them, then remind them the night before and the morning of the appointment. That usually works, but every now and then, they still forget. (I think they act like they have forgotten when, in fact, they actually don't want to go. They just don't want to tell me.) On those days, getting them to move is like pouring molasses on a cold winter day.

S-L-O-W!

Yesterday, Momma was dressed for her appointment but with no shoes on. Her hair was half combed, she couldn't find the right jacket, and she hadn't taken her medicine either. Not to mention, she also walked out without the cane. I told her that she mustn't need it if she keeps walking out without it. Momma chuckled while not even attempting to look for it. I unlocked the house to find the cane and waited for her to get into the car safely, but by the time I'd put the keys in the ignition, I realized she didn't have her glasses. So, I unlocked the house again to retrieve the glasses only to find that she'd left her cellphone as well. Then, we tried it again. All while she's sitting there in the car ain't worried about nothing!

On these days, the extra time also allows me to drive more slowly. It allows Momma to see things she rarely sees now because she hardly ever leaves our street. I even do this with Daddy, although he drives the neighborhood daily. Every now and then, I pick her up in "her" car. When I do, Momma nods in agreement with it and smiles as she remembers things she did and places she frequented when she still drove.

I've learned to slow down and be grateful for these moments.

I can remember rushing Momma to get ready to leave for the appointment because I hadn't allowed enough time. It caused Momma to be disoriented and thrown off because I had made her nervous by rushing her. She couldn't think and even cried because it highlighted her deficiencies. She felt like she was being an inconvenience to me and cried more. Initially, I was mad because I felt she needed to try harder. We were not going to get to the doctor's office until after the little grace period had expired, and they were not going to see her. I called ahead, and they offered us grace. Thank God for grace. Then, I regrouped. I noticed what I had done to her. I realized that she was doing the best she could, and I had caused distress. I had made things much worse and caused her anxiety about doctor's visits. I vowed to avoid doing that ever again.

Seeing the Signs

Do your best to fulfill the seniors' requests promptly. You just never know why it's so important.

So, Ruby Duby had ANOTHER cool whip bowl. This one had a lid on it. She'd been going outside across the street (I'm sure in her house dress), picking the few pecans still left over there. She'd been cracking and picking out those pecans in this cool whip bowl for a couple of weeks. I was surprised to find out the pecans were for ME! I needed them to make some sand tarts. After finding the old recipe that we used all the time, I snapped a picture of it and took note of the ingredients.

After about a week, I made them and took them to her. She happened to be standing in the door when I brought them to her in that exact cool whip bowl she'd given me. We walked into the living room, where she opened the bowl to pull out a sand tart to eat. The look of happiness and enjoyment on her face was priceless. It melted my heart. Her face softened as she appeared to drift back to a different time. I can only imagine which memory that taste brought to the surface for her because the recipe was dated 1967.

Before the night was out, she and Daddy had eaten them all. A couple of days later, I made more, but they didn't make it out of our house to theirs thanks to my husband. So, I made even more some days later and let her know. She asked when I'd bring them to her. I told her that it would be later that night or the next day because I had physical therapy and a long meeting. She told me to "Hurry up and bring them!" in her soft but stern voice, followed by a giggle. It was lunchtime, so I regrouped to get them to her ASAP. I asked her to meet me outside and took them to her. She stood on the steps and immediately removed the foil (not holding on to the rail, so I'm shouting to her from the car to to go on inside) and began to eat them. After taking her first bite, she did the little shake and shiver thing that she does when Daddy sings a certain extra spirit-filled way in church. I smiled and yelled uncontrollably louder for her to hurry up and go inside again. She nodded while slowly turning around and shakingly opening the screen door, making sure to secure the sand tarts.

Sand tarts are simple, yet very delicious little cookies shaped like a sickle cell or a half-moon. They are made of butter, flour, vanilla flavor, powdered sugar, and finely chopped pecans. The taste of the sand tart is similar to a pecan sandie, but better (in my opnion). The sand tart recipe of Momma's that I found when she requested them was dated 1967 (4 years before I was born). I don't know how often Momma made them before we were born, but I do know that we made them often when my brother and I were younger. I particularly remember making them around Christmas time and during the fall and winter months. They are so delicious!

Sand Tarts Recipe

- 2 Tablespoons powdered sugar
- 1 cup Flour
- 1 teaspoon pure vanilla flavor
- 1 stick of room temperature butter
- 1 cup finely chopped pecans
- More powdered sugar to cover cooked sand tarts

- Preheat the oven to 300 degrees Fahrenheit
- Mix all ingredients except pecans until the mixture becomes stiff.
- Then add pecans.
- Shape the sand tarts like a half-moon.
- Cook for 25 to 35 minutes until lightly brown.
- While hot, gently cover them in powdered sugar.

Seeing the Signs

While we can't protect our seniors from all that we wish we could, we can be thoughtful of and compassionate to them.

Mom lost her dear sister in late February 2021. After Harriott (Auntie's daughter) called, I knew I needed to get home to tell Momma the news in person.

I think it was about 10:15 or 10:30 am when I made it there. I'm not exactly sure. Neither the television nor the radio was on. If the tv wasn't on, they would typically be listening to Rip Daniels' "It's a New Day" radio show. But, not this day. They were awake and had been awake. They may have been chit-chatting. Of course, they were still in the bed and just grinning away. "Hey, dawlin'!" said Momma. "Hey, doc!" said Daddy. I told them they were laid up like they were on vacation somewhere, and Momma chuckled while Daddy grunted. I checked her cell phone to see if anybody had called to determine how to break the news to her.

I kept replaying in my head how I'd messed up before. After I graduated from high school, I called Momma while she was at work at Aunt Rosilyn's Beauty Salon to tell her about her baby brother's passing. She'd been talking about Uncle Rufus all that week and even shared the story of how she bought him from her parents for a nickel because he was so precious to her. One of the sisters had called with the horrible news, and I knew I had to tell Momma immediately. Daddy was shaving - if you know him, then you know that was a long, meticulous ordeal that mustn't be disturbed. So, I had to tell her. I remember her screaming and dropping the phone. I felt helpless and horrible because I wasn't there to help her.

I wanted to avoid a mishap like that again. So, I drove there quickly. I broke the news, and with no top dentures in her mouth, she gasped with her mouth wide open and let out a soft sound of horrible surprise. Daddy grunted and "oohed" while carefully and sweetly "eyeballing" Momma. You've got to know him to understand the "eyeballing." Daddy has this distinct way of looking at you that shows most of his eyeball. This day, it was a look of compassion and concern. Other days, it can be a sign to straighten up or indicate that whatever is going on is not as funny to him as it may be to us. No one moved for at least two minutes.

Then I broke the silence by asking Momma, "Where are your teeth?" She laughed, opened her mouth wide to show me the bottom teeth, and said, "Right here AND in the bathroom." We laughed, and I talked about her having too much junk around her side of the bed while Daddy agreed as if he hadn't turned the loveseat into his changing room.

I prompted her to get up to get her teeth, check her blood sugar, and take her medicine. She was sad. She sat with her head down for a bit while on the toilet. I just wondered what was going through her mind. I didn't dare ask her. I gave her her pill pack, elbow bumped her and gave her some time to herself.

My brother drove in from Killeen, Texas, to attend the service. Since we were still in the middle of a pandemic, I was still debating whether or not to take Momma and Daddy to the funeral with so many people in attendance. Momma repeatedly called me asking about the service. I think this was the sign I was waiting for. The urgency and the command in her voice let me know that she was going to her sister's service if she had to walk to Columbia, Mississippi. She was not going to miss it. As a precautionary measure, we decided to go on Thursday for the viewing instead of going on Friday for the funeral to reduce the exposure to so many people. As we neared the funeral home, I began the "how to act once we get there" talk and told her that she was about to see individuals she hadn't seen in a while and would want to hug them, but that wouldn't be a good idea because of COVID19. She nodded that she understood. She just nodded to shut me up because as she stepped closer to the door of the funeral home and saw her sisters and brothers-in-law, she immediately lifted her arms to hug and kept hugging all the way to the casket.

I'm glad we took her. Because my brother was in town, she didn't spend as much time thinking about Aunt Georgia's passing. Tigar had her cooking and cleaning. Several days and weeks after that, Momma mentioned that we would need to visit and check on Uncle Gene (Aunt Georgia's husband). She was worried about him. I can tell that she was also thinking more about how inevitable death is and was grateful to be part of the land of the living.

Remember to be thoughtful and compassionate to your seniors.

Seeing the Signs

Make instructions clear and check for understanding. I guess.

I gathered my plant up after Dionne (a dear friend and trusted staff member) said, "You need to take that plant to Ms. Ruby." I sat the plant on Momma's table that had on it a mound of mail, a piece of a sleeve of crackers, her manicure tools, and her glucose meter. I asked her to re-pot the plant for me. She looked at it closely and asked if I had a pot for it. She insisted on me locating a pot of on my own instead of her finding one of the many she had. I grabbed one from the yard and emptied the dirt from it to give to her. By this time, she had gone to the bathroom, and it was just Daddy and me in the living room. Daddy hears everything AND nothing at the same time. So, I told Daddy to discard the Valentine's Day flowers still on the table when he takes out the trash. Well, my plant ended up in the trash can as well by the time I got to my house to start my sorority meeting.

Mom called right as my meeting started. I muted myself and answered her call. She asked me what I wanted her to do with the plant I'd dropped off as she'd quickly forgotten what I'd requested (so, I'd thought). I reminded her that I wanted her to re-pot the plant. She then told me that Daddy threw my plant in the garbage can. I told her to tell him to get my plant out of the trash can. Instead of telling him that, she just handed him the phone. After I told him that (in a much nicer way because he is still my Daddy and doesn't play), he grunted, said something, and I guess he went to get it out of the trash can.

He thought I wanted him to throw all the new plants out. He should have known better than that because one-time years ago, he got a little irritated with Momma's plants in the yard. They were in his way when he mowed the lawn. So, he took the weed eater and whacked all her plants in front of the house. She was so mad at him that she cried, and Momma isn't a crier, like me. Then, he put his foot in his mouth by saying how he'd asked her to move the plants out of his way. Well, she was so mad that she couldn't even talk to him. She was too angry to cook for three days. By the second day, he'd begun to feel remorseful or hungry.

The plant was recovered from the trash can and looked better. She is "making up her mind" to re-pot the plan as she isn't confident in her ability to re-pot plants anymore. She gave it more life by watering it, pruning it, adding more soil, and whispering to it.

TIPS

- Give instructions while ensuring eye contact.

- Repeat instructions.
- Ask them to repeat the instructions.
- Wait a bit and ask them to repeat instructions again.
- Write down instructions and have them read the instructions aloud.
- Keep instructions short and simple.

Seeing the Signs

Share as much as possible regarding behavior changes during doctors' visits. Those behaviors can be signs and symptoms that the doctor recognizes, and you don't.

We have always loved ice cream and always had ice cream in the house when we were growing up. Momma and Daddy's favorite was Brown's Velvet Black Walnut. Now, Momma and Daddy love Blue Bell's Homemade Vanilla.

During Momma's last appointment, I told the doctor that I'd discovered that Momma had been eating ice cream for breakfast, snacks, and lunch on some days. She even had Daddy eating it for a snack and lunch on those days. Momma didn't like me telling that to Dr. Alexander and gave me a stern, disapproving look. After the doctor told Momma that it wasn't good for her to eat a lot of ice cream, she began to ask questions that led to an adjustment to Momma's medicine.

Questions:

Ms. Ruby, are you hungry sometimes? Is that why you're eating the ice cream? Does your low glucose reading occur after taking insulin the day before and not eating until late the next day? Are you getting up earlier to eat, as we discussed before?

Well, when Tigar came to visit last week, Momma gave him a grocery list that included ice cream. Some way, Tigar and I got to talking about Momma, the ice cream, and what Dr. Alexander said and did. Tigar exclaimed that he'd told Momma he felt like he was being tricked because the ice cream was on the list AND that she'd eaten three servings (small servings, but three still) the day he bought it. Mrs. Ruby Daniel just kept walking to her seat on the sofa as if we weren't even talking about her until I suggested that we throw the rest of the ice cream away. She spoke up by telling us that this wasn't a good idea. Well, Tigar was a gangster (like his Momma) and threw the rest of the ice cream away before he left to go back home. I didn't see him do it, but she told me how upset she was about him throwing it away.

(She's been eating the ice cream in a coffee cup. I guess to make it easier to carry.)

R–E–S–P–E–C–T

Although it was a little cool yesterday, it has been warming up, and it's been staying daylight longer. So, I've been prepping mom to get ready to go walking in the afternoon. She's been mostly agreeable except when we expected stormy weather the other afternoon/evening. I told her that she could get up that morning to go instead of waiting to go with me that afternoon. "Okay!" I said to her, "You are not even going to try to get up in the morning to go." She laughed and looked me square in the eyes and said "No" just as calmly as she said "Okay."

Since it was too cool to walk, I invited her to ride with me to get chocolate from the Chocolate Box at the Golden Nugget Casino.

I'd told her to let me know when she was dressed and ready, and I'd pick her up. I decided not to wait. When I got there, I found Daddy was dressed and cute but wasn't interested in joining us girls. He probably had a couple of more neighborhood loops to make before the day was over.

After Daddy and I chatted for a bit, he asked if she knew I was there. I got to her just in time as she was pulling the turquoise polo-style shirt on with that black church skirt with turquoise and white swirls. I said, "Nope!" She didn't even challenge me or give me a look that time. She just tossed the shirt on the bed. Then, we began our search for a matching and appropriate top amongst the mounds of clothing on the guest bed and those hanging on the doors. She put on her knee-hi pantyhose (the skirt was long enough that you couldn't tell until she sat down) and dusted off some black shoes I'd never seen before. I found her hair pick to give to her to re-comb her hair since I made her mess it up with the changing of the shirts. I grabbed her glasses that she'd sat on the dresser and ensured that she had a warm enough sweater because she gets cold quickly.

We made our way to our destination. We took the escalator even though Muhammad cautioned against it. We almost had a slip up because she was being "observant" because she was looking around instead of looking where she was going as she got on and off the first escalator. We held each other tightly as we made it up and off the next escalator.

We ordered our chocolate candy as she tried to find $5 to pay for her candy in her purse full of wadded paper towels and tissues. I guess she didn't want to use one of the $20 bills I'd just passed to her while in the truck before pulling off from the house. I told her to "close that up" before we had to clean all the tissues off the floor. She giggled and zipped her purse back up. We got our chocolate and made our way back to the escalator after trying the wrong elevator and headed back to Gulfport.

I decided to go to Rebel Dip to grab a chili cheeseburger, fries, and a banana malt. She had a chili dog, Cajun fries, and banana malt, and we got Daddy a burger, fries, and coke. We always had to get Daddy something. Try not to get him something and see what happens. She enjoyed the visit and, of course, the banana malt. (Remember the ice cream story?)

Traffic was unbelievably heavy as we headed back to the house. There was a wreck that slowed traffic down to a crawl. So, I took advantage of the time and asked her if anyone had told her about the stories I'd been sharing about her and Daddy. She said no while shaking up her malt for another sip. So, I began reading some of the Saturday senior tips that I'd been sharing on social media to her. She alternated between nodding in agreement, looking shocked, laughing heartily, filling in gaps in the stories, and looking at me in a surprised, appreciative way. It felt a little weird telling her some things because until then, she didn't know why I'd done what I did in the way that I had. We laughed and laughed and laughed. "I don't know why I'm laughing because that's not funny," she said. "Now the bowl (Ms. Leila Ann dropped off to replace the cool whip bowl) makes sense," she said. "Ah. Yeah. It makes sense now." I guess a few had mentioned the stories to her, but she didn't have any context until the trip home from the burger joint. We also laughed about the parts of the story that we both remembered, but didn't share on social media.

We laughed some more, and she told me that I should write a book. I told her that I was writing one. I'd begun the process of writing a book about her and Daddy. She nodded in agreement and told me that I would cherish those stories. In other words, those stories would comfort us after she and Daddy were no longer with us to make stories. I'd never thought of it that way.

She turns 80 on Friday the 26th AND Saturday the 27th. Ha! That cracks up Tigar and me. That, too, is a story for another day. I think she's excited about her birthday; however, she's not enthusiastic about a celebration for it. I think all that matters to her is just to still be here on this side.

Decluttering

Momma is a bit of a packrat. For as long as I can remember, she has always had lots of fabric material around the house because she enjoyed sewing and was once a seamstress. She always had lots of pots and pans because she enjoyed cooking and took great pride in cooking for her family and friends. She was also a thrift store shopper. Although she doesn't get to do so regularly, she really enjoys going to Goodwill, Salvation Army, and the Dog Store. The 'Dog Store' was what the kids she kept called the Humane Society. Within our local Humane Society was a thrift store as well as animals for adoption. The children that Momma kept loved to go to the Dog Store because they could get shoes and an opportunity to play with the animals. Momma would buy stuff for everyone. If you were moving into a new apartment or home, she'd find pots and pans for you, lamps, vases, etc. She'd purchase pots and pans when there was no immediate need just because someone might need them at some point. She was often right as she still is and would always buy some kind of sweater, jacket, and flip-flops for everybody.

One day, I noticed that Daddy had on a black windbreaker that I knew he didn't buy. It had a megaphone on it. I immediately started laughing and asking him if he knew he was wearing a cheerleader jacket. He immediately took it off while looking at Momma, who just looked like "the bear hadn't been scratched" (as she would say). Then, I told her that she had my Daddy out looking foul with a cheerleader jacket on. All because she was just buying a bunch of unnecessary stuff from the thrift store. She thought it was hilarious. I knew she wasn't going to get rid of the jacket with the megaphone, and she would end up wearing it. Otherwise, Daddy would accidentally pick it up again. So, I discarded it to her disappointment.

After Momma came home from rehabilitation from her stroke and began some rehabilitation at home, one of the therapists cautioned us about the stuff around the house that could be trip hazards. So, my brother told Momma that we would pack up all those shoes and items and take them back to where she'd got them from - Goodwill. We ALL got a good laugh out of that. We began doing just that. She was resistant about letting some things go, and we backed off to concentrate on other things. We told her to go through her things and choose what she was willing to get rid of, and to our surprise, she did. They still have way more stuff than should be safely kept in the house. Instead of just throwing items in the trash or dropping them off at Goodwill, we came up with a different approach. We chose to devise a plan, discuss it with Momma as Daddy doesn't care much, and let her think about it before moving with her consent. That seems to work better. I used to just throw stuff away, only for her to grab it from the trash bin and sit it in another corner. She wouldn't hesitate to give me the "I dare you to touch it" look. I've decided that it was more about how I did it instead of what I did or discarded. I think she felt disrespected and disregarded. Now that I think back on it, I would have felt disrespected and disregarded, too.

I–N–D–E–P–E–N–D–E–N–T

My parents are very independent. Probably more independent than they should be. Experience has taught me that there is a fine line between helping them and disrupting them. I recognize that there is a time for both and don't mind causing a disruption if necessary. Though, I choose my battles wisely.

A battle for independence with Ruby goes something like this…

"Hey, Rube. Do you need help getting a bath?" I was waiting for a response as she slowly strolled to the bathroom with her walking stick. Her stroll was one of confidence…a little too much confidence. She was still dressed in her green and white house dress that snapped in the front. Under that house dress was a nightgown, and who knows what else. Her head was adorned with that black bonnet whose purpose is unknown (to me) because she is not trying to protect her hairstyle (we laugh about it). She also had on a pair of Daddy's big socks drooping down her little ankles. When she began rounding the buffet in the dining room to enter the hallway to the bathroom, she responded. She shook her head and gave me a low but emphatic "NO" without pausing or even looking at me. I just said OKAY and continued gathering and discarding stuff in the kitchen and fetched the vacuum cleaner to vacuum the rug in the living room.

Before starting the vacuum, I checked in on her in the bathroom and at the perfect time. She had finished bathing and was trying to get out of the tub. She held on to the side rail but couldn't pull herself up. She asked for help as she struggled to keep her balance. I ran over and grabbed her but decided to help her sit on the side of the tub and let her work out the rest so she could maintain a sense of independence. I really wanted to yank her up and out of the tub, dry her off, and put her clothes on. But that would have done something to her that I can't explain. (She would have fought it anyway.)

She values her independence. I respect that!

Seeing the Signs

Be patient because being impatient and in a hurry stresses them.

"Stop yelling at me, Butch!"

This has become one of those things that Muhammad shouts out to me when he thinks I'm being too serious with him, and my voice is escalating. It makes us laugh and breaks the tension. He believes that it is funnier than I do and always laughs more hysterically than I do.

One day Muhammad and I were picking up Momma and Daddy from their home to take them to the Gulfport Sports Hall of Fame with us to see our neighbor, Gary, be inducted into the Gulfport Sports Hall of Fame for being part of the Gulfport Admirals Basketball 40 and 0 team and other his skillful basketball endeavors. We were, at this time, not allowing extra time and were trying to be patient with my parents. Daddy was walking Momma to the car and was trying to figure out if he'd locked the door while Momma, his secretary, was trying to assist him and figure out if she'd packed her cell phone in her purse instead of getting completely seated in the vehicle and fastening the seat belt as he had instructed her to do. So, he said with an elevated voice, "Awhh, come on, honey! Get on in!" To which she retorted as she paused and looked at him sternly, "Stop yelling at me, Butch!" It took all that Muhammad could muster up to keep from laughing aloud. I lovingly scolded them as Muhammad and I tend to do to our parents just to remind them that there would be no acting out or arguing during our outing.

During this time, Momma's voice was still very soft and low. We often could barely hear or understand her. We would often ask her to speak up and repeat herself. She would frequently get frustrated with our failure to understand or hear what she said. The speech therapist was working with her at the time and was eventually very instrumental in helping Momma.

As soon as we dropped Momma and Daddy off at the house, Muhammad burst out in laughter and said, "Your Momma's voice was strong when she said, 'Stop yelling at me, Butch!'" Muhammad thought that was so funny and continued to mention it a few times that night before we turned in for the night.

At least once a month, Muhammad shouts it out to me to get a chuckle. Although I laugh with him sometimes, it is a reminder to me to be patient and allow extra time to pick up and drop off my parents.

Seeing the Signs

Be Gentle with Correction

As I have been pulling these stories together and adding additional background information, I have been forced to revisit August 2016 when Momma had her stroke, along with the sadness and struggle it brought.

Speak up and out about medical diagnoses that don't align with what the senior describes and what you see in them.

Muhammad and I were traveling when Momma called on that Saturday morning to tell me she thought she was having a stroke. After going to the ER with weakness on one side of her body, she was sent back home with the diagnosis of dehydration. Once home, the symptoms got worse, and she experienced trouble standing, sitting, and walking. After talking to Tomeaca (neighbor nurse) about the dehydration diagnosis and calling Dana to step in for me, they went back to the emergency room and insisted on getting additional tests and demanded to get a cat scan. From that, they concluded that she did recently have a stroke and showed signs of having prior mini strokes. That explained what might have happened several years before when she thought she had a stroke when her mouth was twisted. She was diagnosed then with Bell's Palsy. I wish I would have challenged that diagnosis then or asked more questions. We could have possibly prevented the big stroke and our current situation.

    Ask questions, listen for understanding, and ask your senior and medical staff for more information until things make sense to you. Don't feel bad about getting a second or third opinion or about the numerous questions you may have.

Priorities

Most of the time, I just want to get done what I need to get done so I can move on to the next thing on my list. However, I can't really do that when I'm assisting in the management of someone else's life. They should have some say so, right?

Well, Daddy had an appointment with the oral surgeon. We'd discussed it days in advance. I'd invited Momma to go with us to get her out of the house for a bit.

Dana, my best friend, called to tell me that she was buying Momma a fish plate for lunch and that Daddy didn't want a plate. She mentioned that Daddy was at Dana's pastor's car detail shop where the food truck was preparing the fish plate and his truck wouldn't start. After I gathered all the facts to understand what was happening, I told her that I was getting ready to pick him up for an appointment and would be able to check on him to see what was happening with the truck. I also let her know I'd come to get him from the detail shop and take the plate to Momma.

Momma remembered the appointment and the plan because she was dressed in her workout clothes, pantyhose, and casual black shoes. I asked her why she wore workout gear, knee highs, and casual shoes. After looking up at me in a disapproving way, she first said, "I don't have on knee-highs!" I said, "Okay, pantyhose!" to which she nodded in approval and replied that she WASN'T wearing workout clothes because she WASN'T going to be working out. Whew... "Momma, sit down and eat your food while I go find a pair of your tennis shoes."

Daddy was ready, too. Well, almost. He was at the car detail shop with his truck. The truck was ready to go, but it wouldn't crank. I was concerned about his appointment because it took months to book it, but he was worried about getting his truck cranked and back home. He also wanted to go by the bank to get cash. None of the things on his list were on my list. On top of that, I was hoping to go back to the office to finish up some work I'd started.

I picked him up from the car detailer and took him home to find Mr. Vernon, his neighbor and "personal mechanic." We didn't find Mr. Vernon before it was time to go, but Daddy's secretary (Momma) had put the calls into the mechanic and left a message. After getting Momma situated, I noticed Daddy was missing. He'd gone out back to look for Mr. Vernon. I could see Daddy through the bushes as he walked down the alley behind the house. That was a new one for me. So, I yelled that it was time to go, and he made it on into the house. I helped Momma get her shoes tied up as Daddy took the opportunity to use the restroom. Momma questioned him about what he was about to do, and he exclaimed that he needed to use the bathroom. He did so in a manner that reminded me of Hoke in Driving Miss Daisy when Hoke told Miss Daisy that he knew when he needed to make water. Momma and I laughed as we gathered her phone, purse, and cane to begin our short trek to the car.

We went on to the appointment, and everything went well. We connected with the mechanic on our way and stopped to get something to eat (Daddy couldn't remember if he'd eaten but was pretty sure he'd had his coffee as his secretary rarely forgets to make his coffee), and we made it to the bank. Once we got to the bank, Daddy didn't want to go in and take care of his transactions. He wanted me to go in to do it. I complied with his request, if you can call it that, without any hesitation, because I'd noticed his back was bothering him.

While I didn't make it back to the office, I checked off Daddy's list, got them fed, and returned home in one piece. That's a win!

Seeing the Signs

Listen to that inner voice as it's usually based on something that you've observed or experienced with them before.

On this particular Saturday morning, I called Momma and Daddy to see if they wanted breakfast. They were still in bed and weren't interested in getting up to eat. I knew it was a bit early for them, but I was up cooking breakfast for me and my husband, Muhammad. So, I asked them to give me a call when they were up and ready to eat. I was prepared to receive the call by 11:00, which gave me about an hour and a half to watch tv, scroll social media, and even take a short nap. When I looked at the clock, it was nearly 12:30, and they still hadn't called. I called them using the usual pattern when there was no answer - call the house phone first, then the cell phone, the house phone again, wait a bit for a return call, and call Daddy's cell phone if there was no return call. I couldn't get them and begun preparing breakfast (for them) the second time that morning.

Muhammad was getting ready to go out for his Saturday morning Petey's Bing beverage run to Winn Dixie and agreed to take the breakfast to Momma and Daddy. I neatly packaged the breakfast to keep it warm, so Momma wouldn't have to reheat the eggs for Daddy, who does not like his food cold. The eggs were placed in the small stainless-steel bowl. The grits were in the small pot that they were cooked in. Aunt B's biscuits were neatly wrapped in the foil they were cooked in and placed on top of the ham steak with onion drippings in the slightly larger stainless-steel bowl. These items were placed neatly in the reusable food delivery bag - a black Coach shopping bag with canvas handles. (This really is a labor of love for Muhammad because he is Muslim, a pescatarian, and hates the smell of pork).

Muhammad grabbed the black Coach shopping bag and made sure he had everything I wanted him to deliver. Sometimes I have other items like snacks or clothing that I've purchased for them that I include with the other items for delivery. They're often left on the love seat by the front door or left in the backseat of the truck. He grabbed everything that needed to go to their house and drove straight down the street to their house. (We only live one minute away on the same street).

He let himself in with the keys to their house and didn't find either one of them inside. He yelled out for them but didn't get a response. He noticed that the back door was slightly ajar and went to find them. Momma is sometimes in the garage washing and drying clothes, and Daddy is often sitting out behind the garage, killing ants with the walking cane that he doesn't use to walk. Muhammad went out back to tell them he'd brought the breakfast that I'd sent when he was stopped in his tracks. To his surprise, Momma was laid out on the garage floor and was not moving. He eased down the stairs from the house to head toward her in the garage as he feared the worst. As he got closer to her, she must have heard him, opened her eyes, and smiled as she looked up at him. That's when he called me. I jumped in his car and flew down the street to see what might have happened. Muhammad had been calling Daddy, but his phone was in the house instead of with him as he sat less than 50 feet away from Momma behind the garage. He had no idea what was going on until I beckoned for him. Muhammad was holding Momma up from behind with his arms under her armpits. Her legs were limp and just dangling. Muhammad had a terrified look in his eyes and desperately needed help with her. I quickly ran to the back where Daddy was sitting and humming as he often did and beckoned for him to come help. I yelled that Momma had fallen in the garage and had been there for some time. He jumped up while mumbling and looking perturbed. I started talking to Momma by asking her if she could stand up. She nodded yes with this very pleasant look on her face. It was weirdly pleasant. I could tell she was actually trying to stand up, but she wasn't helping. I then grabbed her from the front and allowed her to lean on me while the three of us dragged her through the backyard and up the backstairs. Once we got to the back stairs, she started grabbing on the rail, making it even more difficult to move her. I'm not sure if she was afraid that she would fall or if she was trying to help. Momma is super strong. So, this grabbing of the rails made it very, very hard to move her. I had to coax her into letting go by looking directly at her and asking her to grab onto me so we could get her in the house. She was still smiling as we made our way across the threshold of the back door when she started grabbing on the doorways. We kept pushing through the back porch, the kitchen, and the dining room until we got to the living room and gently dropped her in her spot on the love seat. Once we did, she began to lean and tumble over to her right side. I pushed away her dining table, stepped over the newspapers and magazines that she had neatly stacked for someone to pick up, and propped her up with her blanket and some towels.

I scanned her glucose sensor on her arm only to find out it was time for a new one. I ran to the kitchen to fix her plate, picked up a new sensor from the buffet in the dining room, and took it to her on the love seat. I gave her the food and told her to begin eating as I changed her sensor and scanned it. After an hour, her glucose was still so low that the meter gave a "low" reading even though I could tell that she was starting to improve or "perk" up, as she would say. She was back to normal and talking after an hour and a half.

Muhammad was traumatized as he thought she was gone. I can't help but think if he hadn't gone down with breakfast when he did, even though they still weren't ready for breakfast, she would have gone into a diabetic coma or would have succumbed to the August heat.

The "bottoming out" seems to stem from taking her insulin the day before and going too long without eating. I've seen it happen before a few times. The doctor and I both have cautioned her and them about staying in bed too long before getting up to get at least a snack. Because of this, I have adjusted her insulin dose when her reading is higher than it should be. Instead of taking 70 units of insulin, she takes only 40 units instead to prevent the bottoming out that occurs when she follows the recommended 70 units.

Seeing the Signs

Keep a Check on Hygiene and Incontinence.

As they age, their hygiene may change for various reasons. They may not bathe as often because they aren't as active. Their sense of smell seems to decline, as does their eyesight. So, they don't smell or see things as they did before to trigger a hygiene check or a bath or shower. It also takes much more effort to bathe than it did before when they were more active and able.

We struggled greatly with Momma's incontinence and the urine smell that followed for a time. It seemed like she was just sitting or lying in bed, counting on the disposable underwear to absorb her waste instead of getting up to go to the bathroom. A few times, the disposable underwear was so full of urine that it leaked to the floor as she walked. One time that I specifically remember was after Hurricane Zeta. Muhammad and I'd walked down to their house from our house to assess any if there was any damage to their house. When we walked in, I immediately noticed a small puddle of water on the front porch floor. I looked up to the ceiling and didn't see a hole or any water damage. After locating Momma in the house, I immediately realized what the wet spot on the front porch floor was. She'd leaked from her disposable underwear onto the floor, her house dress, socks, and house slippers.

Many years before the stroke, Momma was always running to the bathroom. While shopping or traveling, we would have to stop every hour or two to allow her a potty break. Her inability to control her bladder can be attributed to her two pregnancies and two childbirths. As she grew older and slower due to the stroke, she began wearing disposable underwear.

After trying various strategies to get her to go to the bathroom more often to avoid the many leaks occurring, I decided to have a challenging conversation with her. I was very frustrated with cleaning up after her regularly and smelling urine. Many years ago, Momma expressed that she had NO DESIRE to be placed in a nursing home. While standing in the kitchen together, I sternly told her that if she didn't improve, we would be forced to put her in a nursing home where someone could closely tend to her incontinence. She IMMEDIATELY shook her head and replied, "NO! I AM NOT GOING TO THE NURSING HOME!" After several declarations, we worked on a plan of improvement. I listed my three concerns and asked for solutions. Once she gave me solutions, we went to the living room, where I provided her with paper to jot down my issues and her plan of correction. Since then, we have had very few problems like the one we had that perplexed me for those few months.

Be Realistic about Their Abilities and Limitations

Momma strolls very slowly, making it difficult for her to get anywhere quickly (except to see her "honey" when he was in the hospital). Due to this and her weak bladder, she wears disposable undergarments, as many seniors do. She got a little too comfortable wearing them and subsequently didn't take as many trips to the restroom as she should have been. I got very frustrated with cleaning up behind her and trying to curb the behavior. My frustration also escalated because we were struggling to get her to take her medicine regularly.

She has abandoned the old, unacceptable behaviors (for the most part), but she could not remember to take her medicine as I'd hoped. Still, I took it as a win. I compliment her with high-fives on her success often to encourage her to keep it up and just because I'm proud of her. Because she could no longer manage her medications as I'd hoped, I took it off her plate which eliminated some frustration and fluctuations in mood and glucose levels. I realized that her memory would not allow her to remember to take her medications consistently. So, without a discussion, I decided to take over the management of her medicine and later Daddy's medicine as well. I leave work daily in the morning to give them their medicine and began administering their evening medicine until Muhammad volunteered to accept the evening nurse duties.

Let Them Be

Remember Daddy's visit to the dentist (oral surgeon)? The one Momma joined us on? Well, a couple of weeks after that, we went back for daddy's extractions. I was nervous about Daddy being in pain and being handled too roughly. So, I'd planned to go back with him while they prepped him but wouldn't stay for the procedure. I walked casually with him toward the door after they called his name, but they stopped me. I didn't plan on staying for the extractions as I probably would have passed out. But, I wanted to see them at least prep him for the procedure. So, I sat right back down and was called back 10 minutes later. They'd extracted five teeth and stitched him up that quickly.

The surgeon, the nurse, and Daddy were sitting back like old friends hanging out. The oral surgeon commented on how Daddy handled the procedure like a champ, gave us our instructions, and released us.

I delayed getting Daddy's prescription because I dislike going to Walmart Pharmacy for their prescriptions. The people are really lovely, and some of them ask about Momma and Daddy or comment on Daddy's secretary calling in his prescriptions. However, the lines used to be so long. The wait is long because they are so busy, and it's much farther away than I want.

My delay caused him the same pain I was trying to prevent. So, when his "secretary" called to inform me and to check on the prescription, I jumped up to go to get the medication. I grabbed some over-the-counter meds from my nightstand and took them to him before getting his prescription from Walmart.

By the time I made it home with his prescription, he was no longer in pain and was fine. I felt terrible that I avoided going to Walmart and caused him pain, but he was good. I had to review the doctor's instructions with him again and discourage him from doing what he was doing (spitting) and what I knew he'd do (rinsing). Then, I had to call to remind him AND his "secretary" of the orders because she'd give him a new set of instructions, and he would listen (and then blame her if things went badly).

His mouth healed pretty well, and he was ready for his crowns, partials, etc. He kept asking me when he would get his teeth. Every time I would say the doctor gave him six weeks to heal, Daddy would frown up, shift, and say, "AWHHH, shhh!" He was so aggravated that those teeth were gone. It was difficult for him to eat because he was also missing a couple of teeth from the upper left side. He was probably angry at me, also! So, I just let him vent. Then, I tried to explain the timeline for the remaining procedures…three weeks after the extractions, go for a follow up with the oral surgeon and go for crown impressions, one week later, go for some fitting, two weeks later, get impressions for partial, one to two weeks later get fitted again, etc.

Well, I don't think he was pleased with me because he kept asking when he would get his teeth. He had difficulty eating and was very aggravated and agitated about the whole ordeal.

One Saturday, a couple of weeks after his extractions, I'd prepared breakfast at my house and took it to them. My niece, Mariah, was there at the house as she regularly was on Saturday mornings. Daddy came out of the bathroom to sit in his chair. I handed him his breakfast. Mariah went to warm up the coffee his secretary had prepared for him. He removed the foil from the food and began to eat. Well, I found out that the toilet was leaking again and that he was very aggravated with his lack of teeth as he frowned up, went on a bit of a rant, and arranged his food to eat. Momma looked at him, looked at us, and kept eating in her spot on the love seat while Mariah and I sat across from Daddy, just staring in disbelief.

We let him finish his short rant while he snapped responses to our questions about the toilet and eating without five bottom teeth. He ate half of his food, drank his coffee, and left us in the house because we'd turned on the air conditioning, and it was too cool for him.

This was unusual for Daddy, but we let him rant and have his moment as we worked behind the scenes to correct things that caused him this mood.

Muhammad fixed the toilet, but we can't fix the teeth. He expects me to make the impossible happen and usually exclaims, "Fix it, Doc!" That puts so much pressure on me. But I try to make it happen.

It's Okay to Ask for Help

Monday was a particularly rough day with Momma and Daddy. Actually, this entire week was a bit overwhelming. Managing them and their appointments, in addition to managing my other affairs, almost took me down. I sat in the eye doctor's office and cried a bit on Monday. I don't think anyone noticed. (We were at the eye doctor's office where others were wiping and blotting their eyes also). But I did cry. I could have screamed also. However, I had no time for a full-on pity party because things needed to be done for them, for work, and my other responsibilities.

I made it through, though. I didn't leave anything on the table undone. Daddy made it to his eye appointment on time. His shirt was wrinkled, and he wasn't home ready at the agreed-upon pickup time, but we made it on time. After his appointment, Daddy had to go with me to my meeting. I was late to that meeting, but I was productive and there.

Both of them were ready for Daddy's dental appointment Thursday. (I wanted Momma to go with us just to get her out of the house). She was layered up like it was cool outside, but she was ready. Her cellphone was in her pocket. Her glasses were on her face. She was completely prepared! Daddy was sitting in the house and had already drunk his coffee. He was ready!

The appointment didn't take long, unlike the eye appointment, which ALWAYS takes several hours. They were ready to go back home, but I had other plans for them. I took them out to eat. I watched Daddy look at Momma to tell him what he wanted to eat, even after looking at the menu and listening to my suggestions from the menu. Momma saw him looking at her, but she didn't offer assistance. I guess she was passing the duty to me. We decided together on a burger. Momma had fried chicken (she wasn't too excited about it being boneless but enjoyed it) and a baked sweet potato (which she was super excited about because she LOVES everything sweet potato).

While sitting there with them at the table, I realized it was a much better day than Monday. I also concluded that it's okay to grow tired and frustrated as long as you get back at it.

This journey is unpredictable and challenging at times. I am so glad Momma and Daddy prepared us to endure difficult journeys. They taught us to be tough but compassionate and to be resilient.

Seeing the Signs

Prioritize self-care. If you don't, you will be good to no one, especially those with whose care you are charged.

I'd told Momma and Daddy yesterday morning that we were going to Dana's dinner party and what time I'd scoop them up. They both agreed to attend and repeated to ensure understanding and agreement. I didn't check back on them during the day to remind them as I should have so they could be at home and ready.

When I showed up at the agreed-upon time, Momma was still in her pajamas, and Daddy was in the streets somewhere. Momma was nowhere near being ready quickly. If it had not been my best friend's dinner party we were planning to attend, I'd have left them both. But, I'd had a mini-nap (which I'd tried to talk myself out of instead of going to their house earlier to make sure they were ready. But I needed that nap). So, Momma and I began by picking out clothes and discussing why she hadn't worn the new clothes Tigar and I'd bought (too tight under her little arms). We had to take off Daddy's undershirt that she now thinks is okay for her to wear under her clothing to replace with a camisole. She went to remove that "dang on" bonnet while I searched for a pair of black shoes for her to wear instead of those tennis shoes that are always ready for her to grab.

In between all of that, I was running to the back behind the garage to look for Daddy. He wasn't, and the truck was gone. Muhammad made it there and continued the back-garage search for Daddy. No Daddy. Fifty minutes passed the start time for the dinner. We loaded up to ride to Pass Christian for dinner without pops. We weren't too concerned about a late entrance because if you know Dana, you know why.

When we returned, Daddy questioned us about our whereabouts with this appalled look on his face. This allowed me to address his being gone after we'd discussed it AND his always leaving his cellphone. His face softened because mine must have squinted up too tightly. He threw his hands up and said, "Alright! Alright, Doc! Ooh. I forgot. I do forget sometimes" (or something like that). He tried to pull Muhammad in it, but his diplomatic self said, "My name is Paul, and that's between y'all." They (Daddy, Momma, and Muhammad) laughed hysterically.

Seeing the Signs

Consider doing those things that the seniors used to value when they were more active and cognizant and no longer value.

While sitting in the dentist's office with Daddy, I noticed something I'd seen before but did not see it the way I did that day. He was sitting in the dental chair with his feet propped up. His shoes were barely worn but were dusty and could use a brush and good polish. When we were younger, daddy would stay on us about taking care of our shoes by making sure our shoes were polished and as blemish-free as possible. He not only told us, but he also showed us. We spent time monthly polishing our shoes together. He'd inspect our work before releasing us to do something else that teenagers did for fun. His vision is still pretty decent, according to his last appointment. He does have dry eyes, which cause some temporary vision issues. So, I don't think the neglect of his shoes is due to his vision as I feel is the reason for the lack of tidiness of the house. I think his and Momma's values have changed. However, I'm not sure what has caused the change. I know though that he used to take great pride in caring for his shoes better than he does now, and I should polish them up for him the way he used to do.

The kitchen sink and the bathtub are the cleanest areas of the house. They are sparkling clean most of the time. However, the kitchen floor is always sticky from sugar wasted from Daddy fixing his coffee in the same spot near the stove. In that same area is sometimes food that Momma has unknowingly dropped on the floor while preparing a plate, while cooking one of the few meals she still feels comfortable fixing, or while standing and eating her cornflakes. The decorative rug that sits over the laminate flooring in the living room is typically full of sand tracked into the house from the front yard them and visitors. The rug usually stays full of sand and crumbs until I vacuum it up. A year ago, they were still vacuuming every now and then. Clothes and linen that have been washed, dried, and folded, and sometimes sat on the love seat in Momma's area in the living room or on the side table near the love seat for weeks. None of this bothers them, but it used to bother them.

I'd hinted to Daddy for several weeks to pick up the magnolia leaves in the front yard and clear the sand from the sidewalk. This is something that even a few months ago, he routinely did without a nudge or a hint. He didn't attempt it recently until I showed up to do it myself. Momma helped me a lot but refused to give up any empty flowerpots in the yard except the one small, white ceramic pot that sat inside the huge white rubberish pot that held a perfect pot for tomato plants. Daddy got out of the bed and came out to clean up the magnolia tree leaves when I sat on the porch to catch my breath from clearing the monkey grass from the sidewalk.

They both seem so fragile but are still really tough. They are tougher than me, but not as tough as they used to be. Both rarely complain. When they do, it's typically by a facial expression, grunt, or an awkward movement. I watch how others look at them and react to them when we are out in public. Bystanders look pitifully at Momma and I, especially if they know her and haven't seen her in a couple of years. Men and boys of all ages, sizes, and ethnicities stop what they are doing or slow down to assist us in getting out of the vehicle, opening the door, and gladly move to let us skip the line to the store or restaurant. While she rarely looks up because of pride (I think), she notices everything and every act of kindness.

Change of Scenery

My 85-year-old dear friend came over to have her picture taken for a sorority project. She is a very graceful and refined lady. Although elegant and graceful, she is a little bossy. Her self-proclaimed bossiness entitled her to direct our little photo shoot for our chapter photo project. She and I have an understanding of her bossiness. Every now and then, I nudge her in a different direction as I did on this day. She is often keenly aware of the nudge as she was on this day. She gave me the 'I recognize what you are doing' look and begrudgingly conceded to my direction for the remainder of the photoshoot.

    She continued to sit on the photography stool as we talked about my work (she's a former teacher), her aging and ailments, her recent hospital stay, and her children. I took advantage of this perfect opportunity to document her personality and gracefulness. As I repositioned her, her bossiness returned when she told me in a way that only she could, "I don't want to be recorded." I had no intention of recording her, but I did want to capture her gesticulations—her eyeglasses in her hands, blushing smile, and slight giggle as she mentioned certain things.

Our visits and conversations are often long and very colorful. This day, we laughed more than ever before, and I listened intently as she talked at length about her fragile body, her sharp mind and memory, her parents, and her memories of caring for her parents. The chat included the importance of caring for seniors and respecting how they cared for themselves when they were completely independent. For instance, if they usually slept in late, avoid early morning care if possible. I learned that lesson a couple of years ago when Momma and Daddy released me from breakfast duty.

Right after Momma's return home from stroke rehab, I would go by every morning to cook breakfast before heading to work. They'd get up around 7:00 or 7:30 every morning to eat breakfast UNTIL they let me know that they didn't want to get up that early to eat. I didn't know how to react to that because they were firing me. After thinking about it, I was thrilled about not having to get up as early as I was and not having to go to work every morning smelling like bacon anymore.

My dear friend and I also talked on this day about the importance of checking your demeanor when in your caregiver's role. We acknowledged how your demeanor when caring for them can complicate or enhance the situation.

Seeing the Signs

Know what to do and where to look for funeral planning.

The thought of this was always morbid to me. However, an older friend of mine talked about it freely and comfortably. This troubled me. I could not understand how she could be so comfortable talking about her anticipated demise with a smile on her face. I came to realize later that she was satisfied with the life that she'd lived. She was not only able to raise her three boys, enjoy her grandchildren but contributed significantly of her time and energy to the community. She'd traveled and enjoyed significant friendships of all sorts. While I can't say for sure that her feeling of having lived a full and purposeful life made her so comfortable talking about dying, it shifted my thinking about death and how I approached my commitment as a caregiver. Some of the sadness about the aging process lifted. My thoughts of the aging process being an inevitably cruel faze of life waned. I began to see more beauty than ugliness in the journey of aging due partly to her acceptance of her (our) fate as humans. If I'm truthful about it, I wanted to question God about benefiting a compromised body and a faulty mind.

Because of my conversation with the Grande Dame, I thought back to and replayed the conversation Momma had with me when she was adjusting to her new normal after rehabilitation regarding the documents for their funeral arrangements. I remembered where she told me those documents were in my brother's old room, now the ironing room. I understand that she doesn't want to be cremated and wants her glasses on for the funeral. I probably should have asked questions instead of shutting down the conversation.

Be Observant

Remember when many elderly people were called senile? We rarely hear that term used anymore because dementia is more commonly used instead to describe the condition. Dementia is a degenerative disorder and is often caused by disease or some type of brain injury. Momma's dementia or cognitive impairment developed due to brain damage caused by strokes and aging. The onset of daddy's age-related dementia occurred more slowly over time.

Neither of them has been diagnosed with Alzheimer's, which is one of a few variations and the most common form of dementia.

Dementia can manifest in gait and other physical changes, sensory changes (taste and smell), appearance, personality, behavioral changes, decision-making and organizational ability, memory deficits, etc.

So, as unfortunate as these things are and as disruptive as they can be, they can also be used to work in your favor. Let me give you an example.

Daddy, like me, doesn't really enjoy leftovers. Well...he didn't enjoy leftovers. Momma and Andrea Daniels, on the other hand, can eat whatever, whenever. When Momma would present Daddy with a plate of food leftover from the day before, he would often express his disappointment by contorting his face, blowing air from his mouth, and saying, "Ah, sh...(not the full word, but the sound), I'm tired of this!" Other times, he'd just look at the plate and leave it untouched with the same contorted face, shaking his head without saying a word, not even when asked what was wrong by Tigar or me.

Well, Momma had been preparing Thanksgiving leftovers for Daddy for a few days after Thanksgiving. So, I said to him as I grabbed his empty plate and Pepsi cans from his nightstand...I'm sure you are tired of Thanksgiving food. He immediately perked up in the bed and said, "Thanksgiving food! Where? What?" He was excited by the brief thought of Thanksgiving food. I just shook my head and snickered a bit as I walked to the kitchen to discard the items before heading back to work without saying anything to Momma about serving him leftovers as I'd planned. I'd planned to tell her to discard the rest of that Thanksgiving food so Daddy wouldn't have to eat any more leftovers because we don't like leftovers! But, I didn't mention it to her because Daddy wasn't bothered by it as he didn't remember eating leftovers anyway AND didn't even remember celebrating Thanksgiving.

Because of his dementia, he didn't remember eating the food or the leftover food. Due to his dementia, his (and Momma's) sense of taste is different. Therefore, he only partially knows when he's eating leftovers.

SN: If you have read this far and are 65 or older, thank you very much for sticking with me. Most importantly, don't ignore the signs, and don't be afraid or too proud to ask for help. Ask for help sooner than later!

Dementia

Aging and dementia are very perplexing and intricate. I've come to realize that those affected are not the same; they can, and often do, operate independently of one another. One can be trapped in a fragile body and have a sharp mind, be physically fit and capable with a fragile mind, or exhibit complete fragility in mind and body

I've heard about dementia all of my life and have witnessed it in some form with family members or family friends. Based on my experience, I thought that dementia was a naturally occurring and inevitable part of life and aging. I was surprised to find in my brief research that dementia is not unavoidable as one ages, and it is not a disease, but instead is a collective of symptoms of other diseases or conditions and can possibly be prevented. Although dementia is thought to impact older people significantly, it is seen in a small percentage of those in their mid-60s and only half of persons 80 years old or older (www.webmd.com, 2021). Dementia is generally understood to describe memory loss or mental fog when it is much more than that. Dementia includes diminished capacity for memory, learning, language, and decision making due to damage or disease. This can happen at any age but typically impacts older individuals. Dementia typically progresses over time, usually years, but can also have a very rapid onset for some (www.healthline.com). It involves memory loss, behavioral changes, and personality changes.

The effects of dementia can seem magnified or noticed by loved ones or caretakers on a single day or in a single occurrence as if its onset occurred all at once instead of progressively over time. This dementia exhibited may be in the form of mild to extreme confusion, memory loss, impaired perception, and even delusions (www.medicinenet.com).

As I think back, Momma's dementia was evident a couple of years before the big stroke that caused a more immediate cognitive decline. There were signs of fogginess and confusion that would sometimes appear and leave quickly, before we could process what was happening. Immediately before the major stroke (a few months), Momma displayed extreme aggravation and irritability signs. If I knew what I was witnessing, I could have brought attention to the cognitive and behavioral changes and possibly prevented the big stroke.

Momma's dementia is attributed to the strokes we learned she'd had over the years. This form of dementia is called vascular dementia or post-stroke dementia and occurs in ten percent of dementia cases. It is caused by blocked blood vessels present in stroke victims or those who have experienced brain damage due to injury.

Daddy's dementia origin is a little more difficult to define or pinpoint. I initially attributed his dementia to his age, but I know now that its origin is a little more complex than that. His dementia could be due to the 20+ years of smoking, some other ailment or lifestyle factor, and could be due to aging.

Dementia is not a simple diagnosis. The diagnosis involves several layers of tests and observations. Once changes are observed and presented to a physician or observed by a physician, blood tests, a physical exam, brain scans, a neuropsychological exam, and other tests may be ordered before a doctor can definitively diagnose dementia and its root cause. Diagnosing dementia is complex because of its vast symptoms and varying stages of progression. The stages of dementia can include simply forgetting words or misplacing items (this can also be caused by general aging) to significant memory disturbances such as forgetting the date and time while being unable to figure out the date and time to the most severe stage. This stage includes extreme confusion and the decline of basic activities like walking, speaking, drinking, and controlling bodily functions.

There are several unique types of dementia. These include Alzheimer's disease, vascular dementia, dementia with Lewy bodies, Parkinson's disease, frontotemporal disease, mixed dementia, and a few more rare types of dementia. Alzheimer's disease is the most common form of dementia and affects the majority (60% to 80%) of those with dementia (www.webmd.com). Alzheimer's disease is characterized by the death of brain cells and usually impacts older adults, although the first documented case of Alzheimer's disease was in a 50-year-old German woman in 1906.

It is essential to understand that most dementia cannot be cured or reversed, but the impact of dementia can be slowed with medication. The quality of life of dementia patients can also be increased when family and caretakers learn tips like many of these presented in this book.

According to www.medicine.net, healthy individuals can help keep dementia at bay by being physically active, maintaining a healthy diet, avoiding smoking, and engaging in mind-stimulating games like crossword puzzles. Although doing these things does not guarantee the prevention of dementia, it can help prevent underlying conditions that cause dementia and possibly improve the livelihood of one dealing with dementia. Momma and daddy's cognitive decline differs. They both are aware of their decline, but Daddy will verbally admit it, whereas Momma will only acknowledge it if you bring it to her attention. Daddy seems to be in a haze and very distant more often than not but is attentive, especially to those he is interested in. He's attentive, although his attentiveness is not apparent to strangers. Momma is very alert, obviously attentive most of the time, and misses very little. She sees everything, and Daddy hears most things. They both have lost interest in some things they used to have great interest in. Much of that has to do with their inability to participate as they formerly were able to participate, specifically Momma.

I have noticed that they have days of high cognitive ability, physical ability, and desire. On these days, it is evident in Momma's voice. Her voice is strong these days, and her increased cognitive ability has her engaged in trying to operate more features on her phone and attempting tasks that require more cognition than she typically has.

It's a little different with Daddy now. He is starting to have a few days of decline, whereas Momma has a few days on incline every now and then. Daddy's days of decline involve lethargic behavior, staying in bed all day and not going outside to "sit a spell" behind the garage, the appearance of drooping eyes or bags forming under his eyes, or some discomfort that causes him to grunt or wince when moving from sitting position to standing position or vice versa. He's still alert on these days but is sometimes irritable.

Daddy is pretty easygoing and cooperative even if he decides to fuss about whatever it is one may be encouraging him to do. He has a high pain tolerance and will eat almost anything you put in front of him when he is ready to eat or when you insist that he eats if he hasn't eaten recently. So, when he winces or grunts, I'm concerned even if he says he's okay. During wincing due to pain or discomfort, his dementia is more evident. A few times, I have called to inform him of an appointment using my routine of calling the day before, then again, the morning of to remind him of the appointment, only to arrive to find him either fully dressed or partially dressed but void of the memory of the appointment. Even after reminding him why I was there to pick him up, he seemed to find it difficult to recall what he had recently prepared an hour or two earlier.

On the other hand, Momma may completely forget the many reminders or fully remember most appointment details. Allowing an extra hour before the required departure time for appointments is more helpful for Momma than for Daddy because Momma moves more slowly than Daddy, requires more time to prepare, and demands cognitive massaging before getting ready to go. She needs to know why she's going to the appointment and who she's going to see for the appointment. After getting some understanding, her movement speeds up. I've often watched her move more quickly after gathering some understanding, only to slow down again as confusion set in. Her confusion is regarding what to do next or which task should occur next. Sometimes I offer a gentle nudge of redirection or fetch something she is looking for to quicken the process of getting ready to go. It's sad to see her sitting and holding something in her hand while trying to remember what she intended to do with that object. It's almost as if her brain briefly stops grinding.

Seeing the Signs

Don't ignore the physical and behavioral changes in seniors. They may be signs of medical issues instead of the natural aging processes.

I had noticed that Daddy's fingers were very wrinkled and that he seemed to stumble slightly as he walked every now and then. He even struggled for several minutes getting his right foot in the car one day. I found that a bit odd. His dementia seemed to progress from a mild case to a much more severe case. Momma was even concerned. I noticed her watching him more closely and constantly asking, "How ya' feeling, honey." She'd ask him every 30 minutes, and he would always respond that he was alright and surprisingly not irritated by her constantly asking him if he was okay. I wasn't sure if his lack of irritation was because he hadn't remembered that she'd recently asked the same question or if he was being unusually patient because she was truly concerned.

Also, Daddy had not been eating and was drastically losing weight. I was very concerned as he spent more time in bed and less time outside sitting behind the garage, killing ants, or driving around the neighborhood. I was worried that he would become dehydrated and malnourished from this new behavior. Not only was he not eating, but he would also inform me that he had no desire to eat when I mentioned preparing food or preparing to pick up food. His plates of food delivered to the house for him to eat by the lady we employed to cook a few times a week went untouched. I insisted that he ate whenever we were together. Even then, he would only eat or drink a portion of whatever I gave him. I think all of that led to him becoming weaker and dizzier by the day and caused him to fall as he attempted to get up from the toilet. He became stuck between the toilet and the toilet safety rail. I'm not sure how long he was stuck in that position before Momma realized it and walked up the street to get Lil' Luke to help. By the time the ambulance and I got there, he was sitting on the toilet with his head down and very disoriented. Mrs. Mary, their neighbor, a nurse, was carefully watching him with concern. The EMT and Mrs. Mary confirmed my dehydration suspicion. He told the EMT that he was fine and didn't need to go to the hospital. So, they left him there at home, but I insisted that he go with me to the hospital.

The public relations component of Daddy's hospital stay alone was a big task. I was so surprised and overwhelmed with the communication expected. When Daddy was in the hospital years ago to have his gallbladder removed, I didn't have to do public relations. I guess Momma did it along with the church deacons, maybe. There were certain people we needed to call directly, like his siblings. Some knew about it but still expected a call. Some called the hospital directly to chat with Daddy or anyone of us who answered the phone. Some friends and family expected a daily update or preferred an update every time we received one from the doctor or nurse. My brother and I divided up the communications and sent updates by call, text, Facebook messenger, and Instagram. This was a little overwhelming but understandable because Momma and Daddy have touched so many lives.

After spending Father's Day weekend in the hospital, Daddy was discharged. According to the attending physician, Daddy had been prescribed medication that caused his lack of appetite, dehydration, and the fall that caused the blood clot in his right arm.

Looking for the Unusual

I was there to give Momma and Daddy their medicine and was helping Momma sit up from the bed so she could take her meds and drink the water without making a wet mess. I grabbed her underneath her arm, and she grimaced a bit. I asked her what was wrong with the arm. That's when to my surprise, she told me her arm was sore because she had fallen out of the bed. I was shocked, so I asked for more details. Daddy seemed surprised, too, by his startled grunt. She was amazed that Daddy seemed surprised because he was there when she fell and, according to Momma, mumbled something when he heard her land on the floor. She so casually told me the story and didn't indicate that she was hurt or sore other than the arm I'd grabbed while trying to help her sit up. Both of them are ALWAYS fine when asked.

Rarely do they complain that anything hurts or they have any discomfort. A day later, I noticed two marks on Momma's arm that looked like burns she would often get from cooking. I asked her if she had burned herself because I wasn't aware she had tried to cook anything alone. She told me that those two marks were from her fall from the bed. Now, I'm a little concerned and surprised again. I didn't make a big deal out of it because the small wounds were partially healed. The day after that, while giving them their morning meds at their house, I noticed a bruise on her shoulder that I hadn't seen before. This morning she had on a sleeveless nightgown that she'd not yet covered with her house dress (robe). That bruise, too, was from her fall. The fall that she so casually mentioned was much worse than she indicated, or so I thought, as I found out the next day when I noticed her knees. She was sitting on her loveseat eating the dinner I'd prepared when I spotted the little marks on her knees as I was leaving. There were a handful of small red marks that she told me had, too, come from that fall out of bed. Man!!! That had to be a bigger fall than she made it out to be. Maybe Ms. Pam's gumbo that they were eating made her more forthcoming because she started to share more about the fall as she ate. As she swallowed a spoonful of the gumbo, she said, "I probably stayed on the floor for three hours." "HUH!!??" I stopped moving toward the door and looked at Daddy, who heard everything but didn't act like it and said nothing as he ate the crabs from the bowl of gumbo he had. "WHAT!!?? What do you mean when you said you probably stayed on the floor for three hours?" Momma nodded her head and said, "Yep. When I fell, I just stayed on the floor and probably stayed there for 3 hours." My mouth flew open in shock while they just kept calmly eating. Although Daddy was sitting in his chair right next to her, I asked her if Daddy knew that she was on the floor. He heard me ask it but kept eating and glancing at the tv without responding. Momma nodded her head again and said, "Yep, because he asked me if I needed help getting up." (That had to be accurate because Daddy didn't butt in to correct her). She told him that she didn't need help because she would get up in a minute. So, I was perplexed and needed to know how the fall turned into a 3-hour stay on the floor. When I asked her that, she commented that she just stayed down there because she was comfortable. She told Daddy that she was okay and would get up in a minute. That minute ended up being a longer stay on the floor. Whether it was three hours or not is up for debate because their concept of time is off. It could have been thirty minutes or even three hours. Who knows for sure?

Uncomfortable Conversations

Ugh…I've learned to get comfortable with many conversations with my parents. Do you need help bathing? Did you get under the folds of skin? Is it time to change? Did you poop today? How was your poop? However, there are some things I can't comfortably discuss with them yet.

So, I'm completing the new patient paperwork that asks the same dang on questions for each of the 75 documents with only a couple of different questions on each document. (I'm exaggerating.) I love the offices that have digitized their paperwork or use an electronic system that asks for your name, birthday, list of meds, conditions, etc., only ONCE. Anyway, I'd written Daddy's first name, middle initial sometimes, full middle name other times, last name, birthday, and list of meds along with doses for the 50th time (I'm exaggerating again) when I got to the page that requests….a list of medical conditions. I'm not sure about that. I'm not even sure that I want to know if he has had an issue with his prostate or more issues beyond

GERD and back pain. So, I leave it blank to ask him the questions later when he probably feels like responding to me about it. THEN…it asks, "Are you sexually active?" AH!!!! Nope! There is NO WAY I'm asking Daddy that. I might ask Momma, BUT she will probably say something I'm not ready to hear. So, I'm probably just going to leave that blank and act like I didn't see it. I thought that maybe I would get the nurse or doctor to ask him if they really needed to know the answer, but I would still be in the room when he answered. I would have to step out of the room to let him answer those questions.

After Momma's last fall that she slowly told me about by revealing little facts and several bruises over four days, we decided to move forward with the cameras in the house. (Thank you to all who helped us decide to move forward with the cameras.) I've been cautiously checking in on them through the camera in the bedroom while holding my breath, hoping I don't see anything I shouldn't be observing. Muhammad thinks it's funny! It is NOT funny!

There are some things I don't need to know about my parents. Right?!

Humble Pie

After a series of minor events, I realized a pecking order, an order of importance, so to speak. No! No! There is power and influence that I underestimated.

Since Daddy's four-day stint in the hospital around Father's Day weekend, his behavior had been a bit different. Different good and different, different. Maybe even strange. So, anyway, during the first couple of weeks home from the hospital, he stayed in bed all day long. He wasn't necessarily sleeping the whole day but was "relaxing." He looked better and was more alert and responsive, but he didn't want to get out of bed. By day three, it was time to get up, get cleaned up, sit up to eat properly, and be present.

On this particular day, I tried several strategies. Nothing worked. He basically ignored me and waved me off (away). He won that day because I conceded. However, the next day I brought with me my relentless determination. I was unyielding in my pursuit. I'm not sure which I used…the direct and commanding approach, the soft and pleading method, or the "just stay there in the bed and get bed sores" tactic (I'm not too proud of that), but he did get up. It was a swift 'throw the covers back and sit up on the side of the bed while grunting of irritation' type concession. (Swift for Daddy isn't really swift. His movements are a slow glide that might be defined as graceful and methodical.)

The next day, it was someone else's turn. Mariah, my niece, was in charge of morning meds and breakfast. I was slightly relieved and worried because of his actions the day before. Mariah is and was eager to help because she's an adult now and can TRY to tell Poppa (as she calls him) and Grandma what to do. Whatever she said to him to encourage him to get up had no effect on him at all. So, she called me to "talk" to him because he wasn't listening to her. She knew he wouldn't take the phone to talk, so she put the phone on speaker mode and asked me to tell him to get up. I offered a disclaimer to her that my appeal to him probably wasn't going to work either. After telling him that he needed to get up and reminding him of a few new concerns, he got out of bed, to my surprise. Mariah was convinced that he would listen to me, but I wasn't.

Well…a few days later, I tried to get him up to get a bath so we could change the sheets, get them their meds and get them breakfast. He was so cranky that day that I could have thumped him on the head like Momma used to do to us when we were younger and weren't acting right. He had a comeback for everything I said. "Did YOU have a bath?" "How do you know? Awh," trying to wave me off again.

After several minutes of that, I left him and went to the living room where Momma was walking through after one of her rounds out the front door to check out what was going on outside. She was also probably going to check the mail even though it was too early for the mailman to have run. I told Momma how frustrated I was with her husband (he was her husband instead of my Daddy then) and how he was acting. She seemed to stand a little straighter, and her walk became strengthened as she strolled past me through the dining room, down the hall past the bathroom to the bedroom. I decided to go around through the kitchen and back porch to enter the bedroom through the other door to see what was about to happen. She stood over the bed wearing that green and white duster, looking stern while standing over the bed from her side of the bed, looking over and at Daddy. She stood there with her cane in her right hand, nodded, and said in a gentle but powerful way, "Honey, it's time to get up and get a bath. Her posture was almost normal instead of the little hunched posture she'd developed over the past five years. Daddy's frown softened immediately. His words were still sharp and smart, but not as harsh as they were when he asked me, "Did YOU have a bath?" Momma, still standing erect and confident with her "stick" (cane) in her right hand and her left hand on her hip that made the crumbled pieces of paper towels bulge from her pocket, nodded, and said YES. He looked straight up at her directly in her eyes as she looked down at him and didn't say a word with his mouth. His eyes said that he'd surrendered. At that point, I left them to have that tender moment. It felt like I wasn't supposed to be there for that. Momma's stance didn't change. She meant business, and Daddy knew it. He seemed to understand that this was no time to fight because she was poised to win. As I left the room the same way I entered, I heard her say, "I'm going to go run your water." When I peeked back in on him a few minutes later, he was still in the bed, but he was getting up. Momma was back standing there in the same spot as if she had not left to go run his bathwater.

Daddy threw the covers back just as though he was tired of being in bed and was rising out of bed on his own. He gathered up his coffee cup and saucer and his empty water bottles to take to the kitchen before going to the bathroom, where he'd spend the next hour or so shaving and bathing.

I was in awe of what I witnessed. It hit me while I was processing Momma's move. I realized that she used her influence and power sparingly and strategically. I also realized that I had much less power or influence than I thought I had with Daddy, and Mariah was well aware of her lack of impact. Momma was the "Don." She had all the power and knew when to use it.

The Pecking Order (as I see it):

Momma

Tigar and Muhammad

Me

Mariah

To my surprise, I actually have very little influence. I'm just the muscle and the fixer, and I'm okay with that

Effective Communication

One day last week, during my routine stop to administer my parents their morning medicine, Daddy was awake but still in the bed, and Momma was in the bathtub. I'd walked in like a tornado grabbing the trash from Momma's trash can first, then Daddy's to dump outside and doubling back to replace trash bags. After washing my hands in the kitchen sink and grabbing two bottles of cold water out of the fridge to take to their bedroom along with their medicine, I noticed Daddy was in bed alone. How could I have missed Momma? After I walked Daddy his water and meds, I called out for Momma and heard her response coming from the direction of the bathroom. When I got to the bathroom, the water had completely drained out of the tub, but she was still in the tub. She was reaching for the safety rail to pull herself up and out of the tub. Momma dropped her hands from the rail when I walked in with the medicine. I diverted my eyes to keep from seeing "straight to Chattanooga" and checking my emotions because nothing was blocking my view of her thin, frail body. Momma shifted a bit in the tub either in an attempt to be modest or to get more comfortable but didn't actively try to get up while I was there in the bathroom with her. So, I assumed that she might have needed help and asked her if she did. She immediately responded with a low and emphatic, "No!" So, I said okay and gave her some privacy to work it out, and went back to the dining room where I pondered if I should wait or just go back in to provide her with the medicine before heading back to work. I needed to get back to work but didn't want to leave without seeing her out of the tub. (She does this by herself often without my help. So, I'm not sure why I was so concerned this day.) I went back to the bathroom, where she was slowly and shakily trying again, and interrupted her again. I may have interrupted her because watching my once powerful mother struggle with such a simple task was painful. I scanned her glucose sensor, emptied the pill pack in her hand, and asked a different question after she gulped the water to swallow the four pills. "Momma, do you WANT me to help you?" This question yielded a different response. She nodded and said "yes" this time. I jumped at the chance to assist her.

    I tried grabbing her under her arms over the safety rail, but either the rail or my stomach was in the way. Both were probably in the way. I had no other choice and didn't have much time to spare. So, I stepped into the tub to assist her. I was fully dressed in my sandal heels in a natural hue with skid-resistant soles, coral-colored pants that are a mixture of polyester and spandex, and my loose white polyester top. I was not dressed for the occasion, but the fabric made it possible to complete the task. After getting a big boost from me, Momma was able to gracefully step out of the tub and left me standing there, slightly damp and winded from holding onto her.

Of course, we had to get a little chuckle out of it as we usually do, and I yelled, "Ehh, Rube (Ruby minus the 'y')! Who gone get me out of here?" She halfway turned around with a big smile and made sure I didn't actually need help; then, motioned for and told me to get on out.

It hit me as I walked out of the house that morning. The first time I offered assistance, I didn't ask the question correctly. I tried it again another day and got the same results when I asked if she "needed" help with something. There is clearly a difference between "need" and "want" with Momma. I guess I hadn't paid attention to that before with her, but I think I've got it now.

Celebrate Wins, Big or Small

We spend so much time trying to curb undesirable behavior that we often fail to celebrate but instead breathe a sigh of relief. We should stop, though, and celebrate even small wins.

I woke up exhausted, as if I'd not gotten enough sleep, and immediately checked in on my parents through the security camera app. I didn't see them where I expected to see them. I sat up quickly and grabbed my reading glasses to ensure that I was indeed seeing what I thought I was seeing. It was 6:00 am, and their bed was empty. So, I quickly switched to the living room view and found them sitting in the living room just as they were when I last viewed them the night before. Daddy was still dressed in his Alcorn State University (my and Muhammad's alma mater) sports shirt, dark denim Levi jeans, and his untied Adidas gym shoes with no socks sitting in his chair just as he was the night before. Momma was sitting in her spot on her loveseat with her long navy-blue patterned nightgown covered by her green and white gingham snap front shift house dress with the safety pin strategically placed on the right chest for easy access just as she was the previous night. I'm sure there was a bobby pin (or two or three) tucked in her hair in the front or the side so she could quickly grab it to tickle her ear when needed. (Every now and then, I rub her hair in search of the bobby pin just for fun. It makes us both giggle.)

I checked the time again to make sure it still wasn't nighttime. It wasn't still the previous night. I was confused because it was early AM. I tried to call them and watched them ignore the ringing phone through the app. So, I jumped up to prepare breakfast for them because I was sure they were hungry. While finishing breakfast, I peeked in on them again and was surprised to see that Momma had a plate of food in her lap and Daddy was preparing to get in bed. I drove the food down to them to find they didn't want my breakfast. Daddy said he'd just finished eating, and Momma was still eating. Her plate contained a fried pork chop, fried corn that Momma had shaved off the ears of corn we'd purchased a few days before, and a slice of bread! "WHAT!?" I said. My thought was…We were supposed to cook that together, but she didn't need my help. I was impressed that she successfully prepared such a meal alone, and she was happy that I was proud of her. She cooked everything perfectly and didn't burn anything. I made such a big deal out of it that she was blushing and couldn't stop smiling as she continued to eat. Momma kept smiling really big and nodding her head like, "Yeah, I did that by myself!" She pointed to the kitchen and told me to go fix a plate as I held two foil-covered plates that held the bacon, scrambled eggs, and toast that I'd just prepared for them. I stood there trying to figure out what to do with the breakfast that I'd prepared. Momma rarely turns down food. So, I left one of the plates on the oven and took the other back for my breakfast even though I knew the plate I'd left on the stove would still be sitting in the same spot when I returned later that day. On my way out the door, I kept smiling and looking at her proudly and said, "I see you, Rube (Ruby without the "y")! Good job!" She laughed with cheeks full of pork chops, fried corn, and white bread. I could tell she was already thinking about preparing another meal. Score!!

She did successfully prepare another meal by herself the next day.

Seeing the Signs

Pay attention to their routines and know their behaviors. It will come in handy when they go rogue.

I lost Momma. She wasn't where she was supposed to be. Well...she wasn't where I expected her to be. I arrived at their house around 10:00 am as I usually do to give them their meds. When I made it to the front door, I didn't have to use my key because the door was unlocked, and it was wide open. "Hmm," I thought that was odd, but I was in a hurry to get back to the office. So, I continued into the house to distribute their morning medicine. I walked on in the door, scanned their trash cans to see if they needed emptying; grabbed Daddy's pillbox, Momma's morning pill pack and glucose scanner, cold water out of the fridge (because they like cold water with their medicine - Muhammad recently learned this), scanned the kitchen counter for food that needed to be discarded; and walked the meds and water to the bedroom to give to them. Momma's side of the bed was empty, but Daddy was there waiting. As I dropped his meds in his hand, I asked, "Did you lose your wife?" He responded, "I hope not!"

As he downed his pills, I began to feel uneasy and hurriedly gave him his bottled water to swallow the pills. I walked past the open bathroom door and called for Momma since I didn't see her sitting on the toilet, but there was no answer. I quickly walked outside because now it was evident why the front door was open. SHE WAS OUTSIDE SOMEWHERE, and I had to find her before I left. She was outside doing something she had no business doing because I didn't see her, and she didn't see me. At least, I don't think she did, but I realized that she must have heard me drive up. I started down the stairs to look down the street for her but stopped because I saw her emerge from the south side of the house amongst the bushes. I was relieved to see her and surprised. I smiled at her and yelled with my hands on my hips (because that means I mean business), "Bring your tail out from over there!" She laughed and began picking the branches from Mrs. Mary's bushes that lean over into Momma and Daddy's yard. Both, Momma and Mrs. Mary love plants, flowers, and spending time in the yard. Momma wasn't in a hurry because she was in a place that she loved - outside. She laughed as I continued to try to coax her out of the bushes and into the house. I scolded, "If you'd fallen over there on the side of the house, we wouldn't have found you over there!" I must be a comedian because she continued to laugh and prune the bush instead of following my instructions. Just as I said that, she began to fall back slowly. She continued to fall back until she landed on her little narrow butt. Initially covered by the pink and white gingham house dress, her short light blue nightgown was now sitting up above her knees, almost to the mid-thigh area. The house dress was now covered with dried flower blooms and leaves. I shot down the stairs and rounded the corner to help her up, but not before I had to jump over a flowerpot and around the flower bushes to get to her. Sand and dirt were now all in my sandals and between my toes. Momma's leg was fully adorned with sand. The black house slippers she wore had picked up a little lime green worm as a passenger during the fall, or maybe, she picked it up during her trek through the bushes. As I situated myself behind Momma, I hiked up my navy-blue dress with colorful polka dots, made sure my heels didn't get stuck in the dirt and stooped to grab her under her arms to lift her from the ground. Instead of helping me help her up off the ground, she was picking the leaves and dried blooms (that had fallen on her) off of her house dress. After getting Momma up on her feet, I could then tell why she fell so easily. She was standing on a slight incline by that bush. I had to figure out how to keep her standing upright, keep myself from falling and grab her trusty stick that had landed under the bush from which she was trying to pluck leaves and limbs. I pushed on her butt, shifted my left thigh behind her to balance her, and eased down to pick up the stick while still fussing at her for being her usual, wild, and free self. She continued to laugh as she assured me she wasn't hurt. I dusted off that sandy leg of hers and grabbed leaves that had become mixed in with the crumbled pieces of paper towels that she always kept in her pockets. Once we made it up the stairs and into the house, she and I both sat down and continued to laugh. She had to dust the sand off her hand to hold the medicine I needed to dump into her hands from the pill pack.

 Momma goes outside most days to get the newspaper and check the mail if Daddy hadn't already checked the mail. I wasn't super surprised that I found her outside. She has always enjoyed being outside in the yard and still thinks she can do like she used to do. We just need to find a way she can do it safely or make sure she is supervised.

Don't Beat Yourself Up

I think it's normal to feel frustrated when overwhelmed. It happens to the best of us. For me, managing two households (with the help of my sweet husband) while managing the stressful start of a new school year, during the fourth wave of a pandemic with so much newness mixed with the same old stuff I wish would disappear engulfs me. It makes me feel like I'm drowning sometimes.

It was a Wednesday, and I made it to my 7:00 am doctor's appointment with seven minutes to spare. I heard the nurse say that my blood pressure was a little high. I acted surprised about the dreaded confirmation that my life right then was stressful and spnning a little out of control (and my 50th birthday was a week away). Everything was fine, so I told the physician assistant and the doctor. I wasn't having the esophageal spasms or problems swallowing as I had complained of before. I couldn't even remember if I'd had the Botox injections to my esophagus during my last upper scope when they asked if I thought the injections were still working.

The truth was that my brain was so busy trying to balance all of the other important stuff I'd committed myself to that I'd put myself and my well-being on the back burner. I did not have time to think about myself, which was not good.

The good thing about that day was that I did not wait long to see the doctor and could make it to work before 8:30, just in time for my 8:30 meeting. Whew. The stress.

After checking a few of the million work email messages that I routinely receive and trying to fix some persistently perplexing issues, I left to give my parents their morning meds and nudge Daddy up for his 1:00 dentist appointment. I stuck around their house after administering their meds and serving Daddy his morning coffee because Daddy was moving very slowly, and I needed to make sure he got up to get ready to leave in time to make it to his doctor's appointment. After nearly an hour passed, I insisted that he get up to get ready. He begrudgingly started to rise from the bed but didn't go straight to the bathroom. He, instead, walked his empty coffee cup and saucer to the kitchen, then he started his slow gait to the bathroom to get ready. After another chunk of time passed, I started yelling the current time to him through the bathroom door and encouraged him to hurry up. He responded EVERY time with the question, "What time do we have to be there?"

After eating a tomato sandwich and drinking a Pepsi, Momma went outside to get the newspaper and the mail; then went back to bed. After she heard me yelling at Daddy through the bathroom door, she got up to help me hurry him along. She picked out a set of clothes for him to wear and took them to him after I approved her selection. As I headed back to the living room, I heard her raised voice say, "Butch, stop cleaning that and get dressed." You see,

Daddy has this knack of wiping down the sink and counters and constantly cleaning off his comb as part of his grooming routine. (Muhammad says I do the same thing. Momma does that as well. Maybe Momma taught us all that because Tigar does it also.) By that time, I rounded the corner from the back, yelled at him the current time, and told him that we were running out of time. "Ah, keep your clothes on, Doc!" he said. "Ugh!!!!" I retorted. "I've got my clothes on!" he added, "Well, keep them on!" while he chuckled. I didn't laugh because it was not funny…definitely not as funny as he and Momma thought it was.

I was over it and decided just to sit down and wait. Momma sat down also in the chair that now sits in front of her loveseat. She looked at me, and I looked at her, both with exasperated expressions. Daddy finally walked out of the bathroom dressed only in his gray jeans that showed his boxer shorts because he didn't have on a belt yet and his white undershirt. I knew we were still far from being ready to go. I knew he still needed to pick a pair of shoes, matching socks, and a belt to wear. Then, he'd have to put on his watch, dump his loose change and keys into his right pocket, and comb his hair. I watched him slowly rake the pink comb from the back center nape of his head to the front of his hair, from the back right nape to the front, from the left-back nape to the front, and from the front hairline upward. Then, I watched him do all of that again. Using that same pink comb, he combed his mustache down and across in three sections, then combed the front edge of each eyebrow down with the comb pointing vertically before combing across his eyebrows. He was fully dressed and groomed now…so I thought. He turned around to walk back toward the bathroom for deodorant and to the bedroom for his "skunk oil" (cologne). He wasn't doing things in his regular order because I was rushing him.

I was completely out of patience. Momma was even out of patience. She decided not to say anything else to him. I took my cue from her and held my tongue as well, but I could not control my facial expression. That didn't matter because he was in his own world and wasn't even looking at us or caring about our discomfort.

I could have screamed. We made it to the medical building in good time and waited over an hour before being called to the back. Ah! This added to our frustration. No! It added to MY frustration only because Daddy was unbothered.

While sitting in the waiting room, my friend called to see if we could bring Daddy's truck to pick up some shingles that needed to be returned to the home improvement store. I told her that we'd come after our appointment. We got out of the first appointment in time to make it home for our initial appointment with the home health nurse (Daddy's second appointment of the day and my third appointment).

Josie, the nurse, was familiar with us because she'd worked with Momma after returning home from rehabilitation (due to her stroke). She did the initial questioning and conducted some occupational questioning and activities. The one that bothered me this day and the day they did it with Momma is giving a list of words, discussing something else, and requesting a recall of that list of words. It bothered me before and that day because I couldn't remember the dang on words, and it made me feel like I needed some help recalling things. Josie then told Daddy a story so she could ask him details to recall from the story. As she began to tell the story of Jack and Jill,

Daddy began to look down and drift over to pick up something from his side table instead of listening to the story. Josie skillfully recaptured his attention with her movements while telling the story of Jack and Jill meeting, moving to Chicago, having children, and Jill stopping her work as a stockbroker to raise the children. Daddy successfully responded to her questions without a few long pauses and some deep thought, except one question about Jill and her whereabouts. I guess he was getting tired of it all, so he replied, "I guess Jill went up the hill!" I laughed out loud. Momma laughed out loud, and Daddy chuckled at his own joke. All of us, except Josie, were laughing loudly. She'd missed his joke. After filling her in, Josie, too, laughed.

When Josie prepared to transition to the next set of activities, I asked Daddy what we would do after we were done with that appointment. He replied that we were going to help my friend. He knew which friend when we were sitting in the waiting room at the doctor's office but could not remember which one at that moment. Momma helped jog his memory, and he immediately said, "Oh, yeah!" A few minutes later, I'd ask him again, and he remembered all of the details. However, once we got in the truck to drive to Kim's mom's house, he asked, "Now, where are we going?" He asked that four times within the first ten minutes of our drive. That's the strange thing about dementia. I cannot always pinpoint what he or they will remember and what they will forget. There seems to be some free will, including some decision-making about which information is important to remember and which is not.

I answered Daddy each time he asked where we were going like he'd not asked before. It was like he was stuck in a loop in his head. He tried to remember but was distracted by the traffic and the people. He observed everything, which excited me and scared me as a passenger. His 1979 antique Ford truck has no air conditioning, so it took great effort for me to answer the same question over and over calmly. I was irritated because I was sweating so much that my legs were sticking to the vinyl seats of his nicely restored truck. Even though it was super-hot and humid, hot like only the very southern part of South Mississippi seemed to get, it was a joy to be riding with him and spending that time with him. It also gave me the chance to drop the Apple Airtag in his glove compartment to keep up with him since he still drives often.

Explain Why (sometimes)

My parents were and still are old school parents, disciplinarians who insisted that we did what they said because they said it. Very rarely…well, never did they explain why we needed to do as instructed. If we dared to ask why, the response was, "Because I said so!"

Well, Daddy is not enjoying the home health nurses and therapists that started coming to the house since his hospital stay. I'd told him that the nurse and occupational therapist were coming on this particular day. I'd not told daddy ahead of time that the nurse and therapist would show up because I couldn't keep up with who was calling to schedule visits.

The occupational therapist missed him during the previous visit because Daddy didn't stick around the house. He had gotten up to get dressed in preparation for the therapist's visit that day even though he was not feeling hospitable at all. However, he must have forgotten why he'd gotten dressed and was nowhere to be found when the therapist came. I saw from the security cameras that the therapist was sitting in Daddy's chair chatting with Momma. I watched Momma through the cameras go outside to look for Daddy behind the garage where he often sat, but he was not there. He'd driven off in the truck for one of his trips around the neighborhood or to the store to get his bulk supply of green Freedent gum, I guess. After seeing through the camera, the therapist still sitting in Daddy's chair, I hurried to their house to help locate him. When I got there, it was too late. The therapist was pulling away from the house. Lil' Luke was outside, near the house, and informed me when I inquired that I'd just missed the "doctor," and Daddy had just pulled in around the back.

I did not make a big deal about Daddy missing that visit with the therapist and didn't even tell him that he'd missed his appointment because I knew he'd forgotten. That was happening a lot more often than it used to happen. Because he'd missed the last two visits, this day's appointment was very important.

While at the house for my routine morning visit another day, I mentioned to Daddy that the nurse was coming that day at 11:00 and the occupational therapist would be there at noon. Daddy didn't want to be bothered by visitors and explicitly expressed it as he shifted a bit in frustration, almost in a mini child-like fit. "Ahh, nah! I don't feel like being bothered." I was a little shocked but unbothered by his little tantrum and said what I said again.

He was in bed resting on the left side of his body facing the wall with his grey wife-beater t-shirt (A-shirt or tank) and boxer shorts on. I didn't see the boxer shorts but knew he had them on because that's what he wore to bed with the A-shirt nowadays. He typically wore a regular t-shirt with pajama bottoms when he wasn't wearing what he had that morning. He was partially under the covers with the sheet and the ivory-colored blanket (winter blanket, in my opinion), but no spread or comforter, pulled up under his arms as he laid comfortably on his left side. (For some reason, Momma stopped putting the bedspread on their bed. The bedspread sat on top of a mound of unworn and now too big clothes on the dresser near the foot of their bed close to the back wall.) On Daddy's nightstand was his empty vintage coffee cup sitting on a matching saucer with a used paper towel resting in it near an empty water bottle. Also on the nightstand was his urinal. (It was not empty.)

I grabbed the saucer with the coffee cup from the nightstand to take to the kitchen. There were no dishes in the sink. So, I washed the cup and saucer to keep the sink clear. I decided to save his secretary (Momma) a little work and made Daddy a fresh cup of coffee in the Keurig and took it to him in the bed. He was always grateful to get the coffee in bed. When Momma makes his coffee, he has to get up to get it from the kitchen because Momma can't balance the full cup long enough to walk it to him.

I left the half-full urinal where it was and tried not to look at it. I'd stopped emptying the urinal because Daddy was getting too comfortable with me emptying it, and I prefer not to handle urine. I'd mentioned one time that he needed to do it. He, in turn, suggested that I empty it while laughing sheepishly. Nope!

Although he was drinking his coffee, I could tell his stance on visitors had not changed. I'd heard him loud and clear when he said to me that he didn't feel like being bothered. However, that didn't change anything because the nurse and therapist were still coming to check on him. Although I left to go back to work, I was not confident that he would be prepared to receive his guests.

After I made it back to work, I noticed that he was still in bed. So, I called Momma to ask her to tell Daddy that he needed to get out of bed because the nurse and therapist were coming. I was very busy at work that day and left it up to her to make sure Daddy arose from the bed. When I checked in on them through the cameras, that joker was in bed with the nurse and therapist standing around the bed trying to coax him up. I heard him say, "Ahhh…I'm alright. I'm good." A little chuckle that I knew meant he didn't want any part of what was going on. I was so embarrassed. So, I locked my computer and grabbed my purse to head to my parents' house to get Daddy up from the bed. All I could think about was that dang urinal sitting on the nightstand that contained urine and possibly leftover Pepsi that caused the urine in the urinal to be very dark or leftover water from his water bottle that caused the urine to be very light in color. I couldn't help but think the nurse would think something was wrong with him if the urine looked like it had when I was alarmed a couple of weeks prior only to find out he was dumping the remainder of his Pepsi soda in the urinal. This made his urine very dark or clear if he used leftover water. Either way, you could not visually see what was actually happening.

I knew where the ladies were standing in the room. So, when I got to the house, I thought it was best to enter through the room's back door. I acknowledged them without speaking to them directly and immediately started talking to Daddy, who had now sat up in the bed and had his back turned to the ladies. SMH! I was so embarrassed.

Using a stern voice (and with hand on hip), I told Daddy that I needed him to get up (they'd told him they wanted to see him walk, and he wasn't budging) because they needed to observe and diagnose him correctly. I detailed why he needed to get up and be diagnosed accurately. He listened but did not move. I kept explaining. He processed what I was saying, seemed to appreciate the explanation, and ended his standoff. I sighed and felt relieved because it could have gone the opposite way.

The nurse must have been impressed with what she witnessed because she looked at me with a big grin and said, "I need you to ride around with me the rest of the day!" I smiled and returned to my conversation with Daddy and told him to put on some pants and go to the living room. As I began to reach for the pajama bottoms that were sitting on the dresser across the room from

Daddy to give to him to put on, the nurse and therapist grabbed their bags and white cloth they laid stuff on during visits and stepped around Momma (who was sitting on her side of the bed quietly watching everything go down). With smirks on their faces, one said, "We will be in the living room."

Daddy did get up. He put on the pajama pants that I handed him and went to the bathroom to wash his face, brush his teeth, and commence his hair-combing routine. I reminded him during his routine that he had some ladies waiting on him to come out to see them. They asked him if he'd put his pants on by himself or if he'd had help putting them on. They were surprised to hear that he didn't need any assistance, was still driving, and walked without a cane or walker. They could not assume or even guess any of those things about him by the way he was acting in the bed earlier.

They didn't stay long after that. We were all now comfortable with his diagnosed progress/disposition and keenly aware of his mild to moderate dementia.

Seeing the Signs

Having a positive attitude about your caregiver's role is beneficial to you and to those for whom you care.

    I was late giving them their morning medicine because I had a lengthy web training on a new inventory program. So, I ran into the house to provide them with their medicine. Momma had begun preparing two soup cups of cornbread and milk. That's one of her favorite snacks, meals, and side dishes. I knew Daddy wasn't going to be satisfied with that even though he probably wasn't going to say anything about it UNLESS he was really hungry. Her glucose reading was lower than I'd liked, so I told her to go ahead and eat her cornbread and milk while I ran around the corner to Ms. Audrey's Southern Kitchen to pick up food. It was, however, lunchtime. I stood patiently in line as I must have been the first customer for the day. I patiently waited for them to fetch the server from the back to inform them that customers were waiting. The server was pleasant as I decided which entree and three side items I wanted for my parents. It all looked so good—fried chicken, baked chicken, neckbones, liver and gravy, macaroni and cheese, lima beans, gumbo, collard greens, cream-style corn, fried okra, cornbread, rolls….who could quickly choose. Well, I did because two other customers, then a third came in behind me. One was a friend who immediately asked about Momma and Daddy. I doubled back to get a plate for myself because I felt like they wouldn't be excited about sharing their food with me. Now I had three plates and drinks to carry. I carried them to the car on two trips. I hadn't noticed what kind of mood I was in, but it was obviously noticeable.

I was just trying to take care of my parents by picking up some food they would enjoy when a friend and church member stopped me. Her words that day encouraged me. She didn't just comment on the importance of my caregiving duties, but also mentioned that my attitude about the journey was refreshing and impressive. I had not stopped long enough to notice my mood. You just never know who is watching and is moved by you or your work.

Don't Take Advantage of Them

I'm a little embarrassed by this, but a lot more embarrassed by…just hold on and let me tell you why I was so embarrassed.

Momma and Daddy have become disenchanted with their phones. Momma used to stop everything to answer the phone. Daddy never really embraced his cell phone that we just gave him one Christmas. He only answers the house phone if it is placed next to him, and he is given specific instructions to answer all calls. His cellphone is currently somewhere dead, dead in the living room or on the buffet in the dining room. Momma's cellphone is always charging in the bedroom even when she should have it in her pocket with those crumbled pieces of paper towels while roaming outside.

I've noticed that when I'm there in the mornings, the house phone starts repeatedly ringing around the same time. Momma and Daddy don't budge when the phone rings because they assume the caller is from the middle eastern call center, trying to talk them into buying senior care benefits. So, I decided to get them a voice caller

ID phone system with more handsets than they had. The voice caller ID phone would allow them to hear if one of us or someone important was calling.

I got the phone system from Walmart when I made groceries for both households one Saturday. I unloaded and unpacked the groceries for their house and sat the new phone system in the chair next to the television. Since it was 90 plus degrees outside, I hurried to put the milk in the fridge and allowed Momma to take her time putting up everything else. When I unloaded the car, unpacked the groceries, and redirected Momma with her task, I didn't feel like setting up the phone. I still had to get our groceries to our house and out of the heat. So, I told Momma I'd come back later that afternoon to set up the new phone system. Well, I didn't go back that afternoon like I'd planned and didn't bother to tell her that I wasn't going to make it back. I FIGURED she wasn't going to remember anyway. By that Monday, I still had not installed the phones. So, before heading back to work that Monday morning, I grabbed the box with the phone and opened it. Just looking at the wires and batteries that needed to be unpacked and assembled for the four handsets made me change my mind about setting them up before going back to work. As I shook my head and closed the box up, I told Momma that I'd come by after work to set it up. She was sitting on her loveseat quietly watching me unbox and re-box the system (supervising) and said to me in a low, unassuming voice as she looked down and turned her head to the right and moved her lips in and out as some elderly people do, "That's what you said the other day." I gasped and held my breath in awe for a few seconds as I looked at her undisturbed facial expression and instantly felt embarrassed. I also felt duped. She remembers more than we think she does. She remembers everything from the past but finds it difficult to recall current things…so I thought.

After work that Monday, I drove straight to their house to set up the phones. She is still a little gangster and might try to tap me.

Leveraging Technology

I leverage technology to help me be a more organized and efficient caregiver for my parents. Being organized and efficient provides more time for me to engage in self-care and reduces stress on everyone involved.

Keeping my parents' appointments and all my obligations straight can be a daunting task. To help alleviate some of the stress, I use technology to increase my productivity and manage my time because I work a full-time job, am actively involved in several organizations, and am the primary caregiver for my elderly parents. While there are many applications and devices available for almost any challenge you can think of, I use a few consistently because of the features they offer, along with their relative ease of use. My go-to technologies (aside from my cell phone and smartwatch) include a personal calendar app that is also a time management and scheduling tool, a free note-taking app, and a voice assistant device (with a smart speaker). I use these tools religiously to keep me organized and efficient. I must admit that sometimes a few things still slip through the cracks. I occasionally double book appointments in error because...well, I am human, and I still have not mastered the power of "no."

MY LEVERAGED TECHNOLOGIES

- Calendar app with time management and scheduling features
- Note-taking app
- Voice assistant device with a smart speaker

CALENDAR APP AND VOICE ASSISTANT DEVICE

The calendar app allows me to key in the event (appointment), event time, event location, and add any pertinent notes that I need to remember for the event. (If I am unsure how to get to the event location, directions are conveniently provided within the created calendar event when I enter the address.) I am also able to set notifications to remind me of the event. I often set multiple reminders for each event - a couple of days or hours before the event just in case I get caught up at work and fail to pay attention to the time.

The calendar app is handy for sharing and collaborating with others. Using this app to share events and event information with colleagues and family is effortless. I find it most important to share my personal calendar with my work calendar. Sharing my personal calendar app with my work calendar app keeps all of my events synced and helps me determine my actual availability instead of just my work or personal availability. Many work and organizational meetings fill my calendar and my days so much that I can barely remember my calendar of events without assistance as I used to do.

That's where the voice assistant device helps me. I have a routine set in the app for the device in our bedroom to announce at bedtime my calendar of events for the next day. It both tickles and annoys my husband, but it is very helpful as it prepares me for the upcoming day. (It is helpful to him as well because he doesn't have to ask if or when I have meetings because he hears them announced at bedtime.) The smart speaker also announces any event notifications that I have set in my calendar app to alert me of the upcoming event.

Additionally, my calendar app is set to send me a summary of my daily calendar of events in an early morning email delivered around 5:00 am. This is very helpful as it is usually the first email I check when I get to the office or the first email I check on my phone before leaving the house. Checking this email before other email communications helps me prioritize people and things throughout my day and allows me to see what is on the calendars of key staff members.

NOTE-TAKING APP

The note-taking app has become one of my essential technologies. I use it to write my Saturday Senior Tips, take notes when I don't have a notebook available, keep grocery lists for both households, etc. I also keep notes and information about my parents in one locked (password protected) note on my phone. In this password-protected note within the note-taking app on my phone, I have lists of my parents' old medicines, any new medications prescribed and when they were added, pertinent contact information, login information for bill payments, medical notes from their doctor visits (and mine in a different note), important pictures, etc. My notes are organized by group (parents, work, etc). They are also backed up to the cloud (online storage) to allow me to access the notes on a computer or any device as long as I have internet access (and can remember my login and password). I often share notes like the grocery list with my husband or meeting notes with team members within the note-taking app.

(I also automate as many payments and processes as possible for my parents and me to simplify our lives.)

These technologies are beneficial to me as we care for my parents. Most are available to download or use for free on any digital platform (iOS, Android, Chrome OS, macOS, Windows, etc.) with Internet access.

Calling Velma

I'd reported to my parents' house for Momma's Telehealth appointment (video chatting with the doctor for an appointment instead of going into the doctor's office) to make sure Daddy was up and dressed for his occupational therapy visit. Daddy was ready, and Momma was as ready as she was going to get that day. She'd accessorized her loungewear with earrings. Roxie, the nurse, called my cell phone with the check-in questions and informed me that Dr. Alexander would be calling shortly. I needed to return a call to my friend Velma and decided to do it from the house phone to avoid missing Dr. Alexander's call. I texted Velma to let her know that I'd be calling from my parents' phone so she would answer the call instead of ignoring a call from an unknown number. I moved from the living room where my parents were sitting to the front bedroom so they wouldn't hear ALL of my conversation with Velma. They didn't need to listen to all of that. Velma and I chatted, laughed, and cackled for about ten minutes or so before the awaited video call came in.

The next day Velma sent me a weird text message asking if I was calling her. I wasn't sure what she meant and asked in response if she wanted me to call her…like maybe I'd forgotten we'd scheduled a call OR perhaps she'd incorrectly remembered that I was going to call. So, I called her to get clarification. She explained that she had gotten a call from the same number I'd called her from when we talked while at my parents' house. Before she could finish the statement, another call from that same number was coming in. She paused me to answer the call. In true Velma fashion, she came back to our call giggling and told me it was Ms. Ruby (my mother) who had called both times. Velma began sharing their brief conversation with me, and I began to fill in as she talked because I know Momma so well.

Momma: "Hello!!! HELLO! Who is this?"

Velma: "Ms. Ruby, this is Velma, Tracy's friend."

I chimed in and said…she then said, "Oh!" (a short quick, Oh! that was an octave lower than that loud Hello).

Then…to not be outdone, Momma said: "So…how are you doing?" As if she meant to call her.

This same event and conversation went on multiple times a day for almost a week.

Velma was getting daily "Oh! How are you doing?" calls because Momma was redialing the strange number on her phone and never remembered whose number it was until Velma reminded her. After the reminder, she immediately remembered, but still called an hour or so later. It continued until Muhammad deleted all calls to Velma from their house phone.

My friend, Velma, was so sweet about it and understood why it was happening. I appreciate her for that. So, make sure your friends know. Don't hide your struggle.

SN: I know she calls and FaceTimes some of you all, too. Just be kind to her and patient with her OR don't answer!

Seeing the Signs

Let their gratefulness encourage your role as a caregiver.

I don't always get it right. However, I'm blessed to have parents who don't usually tell me when I don't get it right because they are probably just grateful for my effort during those times. They are always grateful for everything (almost everything) we do for them. (Daddy still doesn't like my prying him out of bed to meet with the nurse and therapists before he's ready to get up on his own.) They ALWAYS say thank you. They may not tell us in the moment of the act, but before we leave them, they thank us. They often tell us, "We don't know what we'd do without y'all!" I usually reply, "Yes, y'all do!" to lighten the mood and stop me from crying. It's the sweetest thing because I can feel the sincerity of their gratefulness oozing from them even before they open their mouths to express it.

Some mornings when I'm passing medicine to them while they are still in bed, Daddy moves from one side of the bed to the other side to pass pills and cold-water bottles and to pick up empty water bottles and his empty coffee cup, just to tell me how pretty I look through a big proud smile. (I think Daddy is more lucid on those days). When that happens, Momma stops snapping the buttons on the house dress she has just put on over her nightgown to look closely at what I'm wearing to see if she agrees with his assessment. She usually agrees. She offers a nod of agreement and a big grin when she does.

Their gratefulness makes the great task of caring for them much easier. I'm aware that they may not always be this way. But I hope we can channel these memories to energize us should the expressions of gratefulness decline or disappear altogether.

That Dang on Truck!!!

―――――――――

Two of my friends and I dusted off 'Take it to the Bridge' Thursday and walked the 'Ocean Springs' bridge like some young whipper-snappers whose hip flexors and ankles weren't ready for the bridge's high rise. Anyway, after dropping Dionne off and grabbing some food from KFC, I drove home only to be met by Muhammad with a strange question. "Did you happen to stop by your parents on the way in?" I was confused. With a furrowed brow, I pondered if I'd forgotten to stop by my parents' house to do something before I responded to Muhammad's question. With a bewildered look, I responded that I had not stopped by there and, in true fashion, asked him, "Why?" (He hates that question from me). He then informed me that when he went to do his night nurse duties, Daddy wasn't there. I was confused and immediately asked if he'd checked for him behind the garage. Muhammad told me that Daddy was not behind the garage and was assumed to be gone in the truck because the truck was not there either. Unlike Muhammad, who was calm (and getting ready to begin his virtual meeting), I started to panic. I dropped the food on the counter and quickly left out of the door to find my Daddy. It was 8:00 pm then, and it was dark, dark. Daddy should have been home. My intuition told me something was wrong. My intuition rarely leads me astray and didn't this time either, as I would learn. I ran to the back of the garage where Daddy normally sat. He wasn't there. I then checked to see if the truck was still gone as Muhammad described, and it was. Full panic mode began to form as I started to question Momma who, after a few questions, remembered asking Daddy to go get her a Big One (large chili cheeseburger) from Ward's. There is a Ward's less than 5 minutes from the house.

A few months ago, I'd dropped the Apple AirTag (tracker device) in the glove compartment of Daddy's truck to assist should we need to find him. I pulled up the "Find My" app on my phone and could not figure out how to access the AirTag because I had started to really panic. I settled down a bit and tapped over to the AirTag that I labeled "Daddy's Truck." It showed where the truck was and that it had been sitting in the same spot in Perkinston for 27 minutes, then 37 minutes... By the time I processed that he was probably broken down on the side of the road, the truck had been there 40 something minutes. Once I understood what I was seeing in the app, I headed for the door to follow the AirTag's directions. It must have clicked for Muhammad, too, about the same time because instead of joining his meeting as he intended, he headed to the barbershop to look for Daddy.

We met up at the Dollar Tree and headed up Highway 49 as quickly as we safely could. I was overwhelmed with "what ifs." What if he started walking home? It would be pretty hard to see him because he's so dark (a beautifully rich dark umber color, but still a very dark man) and wore dark jeans and a plaid shirt. What if someone hit him? What if he can't remember the house phone number? What if he walks away from the truck and gets lost in the woods trying to get help? The more we drove, the more "what ifs" arose. The directions the AirTag provided took us directly to the truck where Daddy was sitting in Perkinston. He was accompanied by some wonderful, helpful, and kind sheriff guys who understood what they were dealing with (dementia).

When we got there, the hood of the truck was up, and Daddy was on one of the sheriff guys' cell phones. "The truck's oil was gone," said the older guy. The truck should not have cranked up at all and definitely should not have been capable of leaving the neighborhood because Tigar (my brother) drained the oil (so he thought) when he was here the previous weekend.

After doing introductions and offering pleasantries with the sheriff guys, we asked Daddy to get out of the truck, so I could jump in to steer it while Muhammad and the deputies pushed it off the road where we left it overnight. Daddy was okay and probably could have driven the truck better than I did. I struggled to turn the steering wheel as they yelled, STRAIGHTEN UP! Straighten up! STRAIGHTEN up!

I was so relieved to see Daddy safe, sound, and calm with caring people who eventually noticed signs of his deficiency. They did call Momma on the house phone, and she did answer the phone a couple of times. I was glad to know Daddy remembered the house phone number since he no longer cared to carry his cell phone. I was also surprised and relieved that Rube answered the phone.

Daddy was grateful to be headed home but was concerned about leaving his truck. At that moment, I didn't care about anything but him. Although I didn't care anything about that dang-on truck right then, I knew I had to contend with getting the truck home. I reassured Daddy that I would take care of the truck. He was comforted but wanted to know where Tigar was to make sure Tigar was aware and in agreement with what was taking place. We called him and talked to him as we drove southbound on Highway 49.

After barely sleeping, I got up to drive back to South Park in Perk to make sure the business where the truck was parked didn't have Daddy's precious truck towed to some unknown location. We got it towed home since Tigar didn't want it towed to an automotive shop. The tow truck guy was so talented and patient that he towed the truck to the back of the house and neatly in the garage like it was when Daddy got in it and shouldn't have.

That Apple AirTag that I bought from Nave (one of my techs) saved the day!!!

I am still emotionally drained by it all. Now Tigar has to get a new motor for the truck and get it fixed. I get to do all the running around to ensure that the truck gets fixed and paid for on Tigar's behalf because he isn't here.

Whew…

Daddy didn't have his cell phone on him, but he had that green Freedent gum in his shirt pocket.

Don't ignore your intuition and use the tools available to you!

WHAT HAD HAPPENED WAS

I'm inquisitive and like to know the "why." Anyway, the dang on truck issue still baffled me a little. I still want to know why he was trying to go somewhere at that time of the evening. (Keep in mind that they have limited concept of the time of day because they are on this perpetual vacation with no worries, a maid, and a couple of nurses.)

I think I know why the dang on truck incident happened. However, parts of the story will remain a mystery to all of us because neither one of them can remember or process it without frustration. Additionally, they often don't remember to share details with the maid (me).

I saw an incoming "No ID" call on my cell phone while sitting at my desk at work. I don't usually answer those calls, but something compelled me to answer this day. To my surprise, it was momma. I immediately asked her which phone she was calling from because I really wanted to know WHY the call was showing up like that. She told me she was calling from her cellphone. Although she told me she was calling from her cell phone, I still don't know which phone she was actually calling from. She still managed to call Velma again a week ago and inadvertently blocked my and Mariah's calls on the house phone.

Back to why Momma called, she asked the same ole question that irks me like my 'Why?' questions irk my sweet husband. "Where you at?" she asked to which I replied, "I'm at work, Momma. What YOU doing?" I could hear her grin while she answered, "I'm talking to you!" We both chuckled, and she got right down to why she was calling. She said, "Daddy, wants you to go get us a Big One (chili cheeseburger from Wards)." I thought that was a weird request from Daddy, but I didn't question it at that moment. It was near the end of the day, so I wrapped up what I was working on and drove to the Ward's closest to the office and ordered the Big Ones (no fries) just as she requested.

Momma isn't a liar, nor does she embellish stories, but Daddy doesn't request Big Ones. That's Momma's thing. Daddy is a whopper guy. (It's all strange because they never wanted fast food when we were younger). Regardless, I got the burgers. I walked in the house with the bag, handed Momma her burger, and went to the bedroom to give daddy his Big One because he wasn't sitting in the living room with Momma. Daddy wasn't in the bedroom, as I assumed. He wasn't anywhere in the house. Of course, when I asked Momma where he was, she shrugged her shoulders and told me she didn't know where he was. Well, he was sitting out back behind the garage, fully dressed like he was going somewhere. I gave him his sandwich that he was surprised to receive and noticed as he reached for it that he had his keys in his hand. As I walked back into the house to grab him a Pepsi and a jacket for him, it hit me. If he had the right keys to the truck and if the truck cranked, he would have gone to try to do what Momma asked of him. Instead, I'm sure he said to her, "Call that girl to go get the Big Ones."

Here's what I think happened the day we used the Apple AirTag to find Daddy and his truck. Momma asked Daddy to go to Wards to get her a Big One. Daddy went to get it, got distracted as his mind wandered, and continually drove up Highway 49 until all the remaining oil ran out of the truck's engine.

I sometimes forget he suffers from dementia until we are going places or getting ready to go somewhere, and he constantly asks where we are going. His brain will not retain those details for longer than a few minutes or until he has been told six or more times if he retains it at all. However, things from years ago flow out with no problem. It's the most fascinating thing to me.

The mystery is still not solved, but it makes more sense.

Be Grateful

I want to thank my husband, niece, and brother. Tigar is in town right now, and it feels like I'm on a mini vacation!

Some time ago, Muhammad volunteered for the night nurse position because he recognized the great task and committed to MOST of this journey. My parents adore him and constantly ask about him when I'm there without him (as if they hadn't just seen him). Well, it's mostly Daddy who asks, "Where is my son-in-law?" OR "How is my son-in-law?" I think Daddy is concerned that I might run him off, and he wants to make sure he has an opportunity to intercede or something before that happens. I don't know.

I don't always communicate as I should with Muhammad about what's going on with my parents, and it sometimes causes him great stress. I often just get so busy checking boxes and don't always communicate in a timely manner. (He's usually very busy, too, but rarely do our busy periods overlap like they have the past couple of months.) Last Saturday (actually, all of last week) was super busy for me. I spoke to this beautiful group of ladies for their Women's Seminar in Pascagoula and dined with several of them afterward. Then, I raced back to Gulfport to set up the lab to host and conduct our chapter's first in-person Grow with Google training.

While I was ending my presentation to the sassy ladies at St Peter's Catholic Church, my niece started calling to request help getting Momma and Daddy ready to go over to the Dickens' house for lunch. Every time I sent her a call to voicemail, she called right back. My vibrating phone could be heard through the mic on the podium. I was a little embarrassed but didn't get that sick feeling that something was wrong either. After signing a few books and taking pictures, I returned Mariah's calls, but those jokers weren't answering any phones. So, I dropped in on the cameras to find them in the house and told them to answer the phone. I suggested a different outfit for Momma and guided Mariah to clothes in the other room. Mariah then wanted me to talk to Daddy because he wouldn't listen to her and wouldn't get up to get dressed. She also needed me to know that they'd been arguing. She walked me in on FaceTime to Daddy so he could see me tell him to get up. I just said, "Hey, Daddy!" and told Mariah to leave him alone instead of insisting that he accept the lunch invitation. She was disappointed that she couldn't witness the magic she thinks happens between daddy and me. She really wants them to act right with her, but they rarely do.

Remember when I said MOST earlier? I mentioned that Muhammad was committed to MOST of my journey. Well, he, unlike Mariah, wants no part of insisting that my parents do something. When he went down to their home one evening, I'd asked him to tell Momma it was time to do what I'd told her she needed to do earlier and to change her loungewear. His approach was to ask her if she was getting ready to put on her pajamas. She gave him a stern and emphatic NO! while looking directly at him (as he told the story). He left it alone and tried to revisit it before returning home, and she said, "NO!" again with what he calls her 'strong voice.' So, he left it alone. (I told him that he let momma punk him. He didn't care. We both just laughed.)

Momma is always down to eat and always down for the company, but Daddy is an introvert like me and would much rather avoid social gatherings even though we do like people. Once Momma was dressed, Mariah took her over to the next street to drop her off at Deacon and Mrs. Dickens' house and a couple of hours later picked her up along with a plate of food for Daddy.

Muhammad didn't know any of these plans and was texting me with concerns while I was dining with the ladies in Pascagoula. I hadn't told him that Gretta had called the day before with the plans. I couldn't commit to helping them get ready or taking them to the lunch date, so I didn't share it with him. He knew I had a busy day and was just going to make sure my parents were alright while I was unavailable. He'd checked in to see if they were up and moving around and noticed that Momma had real clothes on. She had on street clothes, so to speak, and not her usual lounging clothes. Then, he couldn't find her anywhere on the cameras and zipped down the street to check on them. When I could talk, I filled him in on the plans Gretta orchestrated for her parents and my parents, and he could breathe normally.

I am so very grateful for Muhammad, Mariah, and Tigar. Having help is wonderful but having someone who understands the struggle is food for my soul. I share these struggles and laughs because I hope they can feed the souls of others who may, too, be on this journey. I also hope that these Saturday Scribbles help others navigate the journey they are about to embark on instead of having to start blindly as I did.

Let's disrupt the silence and talk about how difficult this journey can be. It's okay.

Conclusion

It was a Friday. I will never forget it.

I watched as a flurry of scenes breezed by the window while sitting in my seat on the Greyhound bus. I was on my way home from my first semester of college and was anxious to see my family.

What I didn't know...in fact, none of us knew just how sick my grandfather had been in the weeks before my journey home. From afar and on the phone, I missed a lot of the "clues" and "behaviors" described in this book. I didn't know that I wasn't getting the whole story or that my grandfather wasn't completely capable of giving it to me.

I wouldn't get a chance to see him. I stayed on the bus beyond my hometown to visit other family first and figured I would see him the next day. It was a decision I have regretted ever since.

Now, whenever dealing with elders, I find myself trying to be alert for clues. Have they eaten? What's their pain level? Is the room cold? Can I tell if they have been taking care of hygiene? Have they been taking their medication?

How can I make their life easier?

Many questions with a plethora of answers are possible. There is no single right answer. The real answer is that there might be many ways to do things. Anyone that has ever had to care for someone else understands that what works one day may not work another day. Then on other days, it may only partially work.

The tips contained within these pages have been useful. They have been, at times, entertaining. They have also sometimes been insightful. What the tips have always been (and I believe I can speak on this considering I was there) is honest. In the moments of the honesty of caregiving, one will find themselves experiencing the gambit of emotions. The success of an elder taking their medicine and being bright and engaged can make you happy, while the frustration of realizing that your loved one isn't the same as they were and never will be...can leave you in tears. Recall the advice Tracy offered about not being shocked about the decline of their physical appearance. Their bodies will continue to change. One of my favorite experiences with her dad was just a couple of years ago when he and I got on the roof of the house to pick oranges from the tree. He laughed and asked me if I was scared. I immediately replied "No" and thought to myself, there is no way in the world I am going to let an 80-year-old man "show me up." Now while I was not scared, I was in awe of the fact that this 80-year-old man was on the roof!

Too many times, we see the meme on social media of an infant and elder looking at each other with the connection of commonality in their eyes. A baby is new to the world and needs love and care. The baby needs someone to make crucial decisions resulting in their ability to live. Everything from food, shelter, medication, and essential life goods are provided for babies, and we don't think twice about it. It's understood that a baby's mind has not grown into the ability to make decisions for themselves. So we make the decisions for them. We understand and accept the idea that a child's brain is not in the state to do these things. But what of our elders?

A common issue within some cultures is the absence of understanding how the decline of an elder's brain and mental acuity can be much like the issues present dealing with a developing baby. While it does not happen with every elder, it can certainly happen to many. It can manifest in simple moments like forgetting where one has placed their keys. Maybe sometimes it's as innocent as a forgotten birthday. But what if it becomes much more than that? What if your elder goes for a drive and finds himself almost an hour away from home, and it's approaching dusk? What does one do then? What action plan can one engage in? What if your elder forgets to turn off the gas on the stove because they were attempting to cook and care for themselves as they always have?

Here, we find the difference between the baby and the elder. The baby does not know how to care for himself, nor will he try. (Only maybe when they reach the "terrible-twos," they might THINK they know what they are doing). Our elders have spent a lifetime taking care of themselves. They even may have had a hand in raising you. How do we care for someone that is used to caring for themselves? How do we position ourselves to gain their trust in such a manner that they allow us to make the necessary decisions for them? How do we get them to turn over the keys to the truck and it not be an issue?

Again, it may not be the same answer for everyone. As we read earlier in the book, sometimes it is crucial to allow the elder/parent to control certain things to relinquish others. That may or may not be the same thing for you. The idea remains that one will have to make some crucial decisions. Much like the example of the baby, these decisions can affect the comfort and quality of life of our elders.

Over the last five years, I have discovered that life can change in the blink of an eye. I have shared moments where there was uncontrollable laughter. Times where I "just slid on down" on the floor laughing. Then there were other times as well. Times unbeknownst to anyone until now that I have gone in the bathroom and cried my eyes out. It was not because of anything to do with the in-laws in the stories you have read within these pages. It was because I wished I had a book like this long ago when I missed certain clues with my grandfather. I wish I had a book like this when I tried to comfort my grandmother, his widow, through her decline, which came within the years following me getting off that bus.

Cherish your role as a caregiver. Embrace all the moments, the highs and lows, as an opportunity to make someone's life better.

Muhammad Hardy

www.ingramcontent.com/pod-product-compliance
Lightning Source LLC
Chambersburg PA
CBHW032045150426
43194CB00006B/424